Mastering the College Application Essay

The **Art** of **Writing** to **Discover**

GLORIA CHUN, PhD

outskirtspress
DENVER, COLORADO

Mastering the College Application Essay
The Art of Writing to Discover
All Rights Reserved.
Copyright © 2014 Gloria Chun, PhD
v3.0

Outskirts Press, Inc.
http://www.outskirtspress.com

ISBN: 978-1-4787-2375-2

Outskirts Press and the "OP" logo are trademarks belonging to Outskirts Press, Inc.

PRINTED IN THE UNITED STATES OF AMERICA

O brave young achievers, you have now achieved the pinnacle
And forgive me if it sounds cynical
But as we gather to celebrate ya and hail ya
It is time to think about the benefits of failya....
Today's grievous mistake is tomorrow's humorous story
    --*Garrison Keillor*, excerpted from the "Address to the
            Harvard Chapter of *Phi Beta Kappa*, June 2008

Table of Contents

A Note to the Reader i
Introduction...iii

I. Get Ready!

Chapter One: Tilting Toward Happiness 1
Chapter Two: Reading to Write 8
Chapter Three: Put up your Antennae 14
Chapter Four: Write What You See 16
Chapter Five: Practice Makes Perfect 20

II. Understanding the Personal Essay

Chapter Six: What Is the Personal Essay?...............................22
Chapter Seven: The Shape of the Personal Essay....................28
Chapter Eight: Interpreting Essay Prompts 33

III. Crafting the Essay

Chapter Nine: Stage One--Brainstorming.............................41
Chapter Ten: Stage Two—First Draft 46
Chapter Eleven: Stage Three—Revision.................................48

IV. Tools for Writing

Chapter Twelve: Elements of Good Writing............................50
Chapter Thirteen: Twenty Most Common Pitfalls in Writing
    the College Application Essay...66
Chapter Fourteen: Winning Essays 70
Bibliography (Works Used) 100

A Note to the Reader

THIS BOOK IS about slow-cooking a habit of mind and an orientation toward writing meant to elicit a powerful response. With the proper mindset, practice, and good writing tips you will write lyrical essays that sets you apart. At the heart of this book is a new approach to writing, closer to the original meaning of *essay*, which in old French means *to examine, probe, or experiment*.

I start with the premise that writing a winning college application essay is hard work but it *can be learned*. Unlike most books on essay writing, it does not promise to deliver your essay in 10 easy steps. In fact your ability to innovate depends on moving beyond thinking that your essay can be written with breezy bullet points as your guide. Rather, this book is meant to elevate the college application essay to what it rightfully is—not your personal statement, a brag sheet, or a narrative resume, but a *personal essay*.

The personal essay is defined in the *Handbook of Literature* as "a kind of informal essay, which utilizes an intimate style, some autobiographical content or interest, and an urbane conversational manner." Graceful, honest, and idiosyncratic, the personal essay is the perfect medium to make a unique imprint. It combines the best elements of fiction and reflection.

Mastering the College Application Essay is organized to

move you through the natural process of writing from developing the right psychological orientation, to brainstorming, to applying literary techniques for shaping your narrative. Whenever possible, I model for you how to pitch your own writing with a deeply engaging personal voice. I invite you to become immersed in the process of thinking through writing.

The names of students mentioned in this book are made-up to guard their privacy, unless I was given explicit permission to use their real names. My students remain the inspiration behind this book.

Introduction

The Relaxed Approach

What would you do with a free afternoon? (Writing Prompt from Yale University Admissions Supplement)

"I'd put on my purple tie, gather some daffodils, and promenade down Camino Diablo, until someone falls in love with me." –Colton Jang (2011 Yale admit)

WHAT IF I told you that the best way to write the college application essay is to become an idler? To become an idler, according to Samuel Johnson, you have to do less and reflect more. Kill the instinct to try and impress the college admissions officer. Instead, demonstrate your appetite for joy. You might be tempted to either close this book and walk away, or more likely--because you are still reading--consider how this paradoxical advice can help unfreeze your writing hand to produce an essay that will get you a second look from the admissions officer.

Telling a college-bound high school student like you to relax before sitting down to write is like telling the passengers to fasten their seatbelts and sit tight as the plane plummets in free fall. When was the last time one of your teachers told you to sit back and relax? High school is synonymous with high stress. The competition to get into college has you constantly on your toes seeking out every available AP class, filling your summers with internships and SAT prep, setting up your charity, developing a new app or writing a book—all on four hours of sleep. In this high-stakes, highly evaluative culture, it is no wonder why many of you might approach the college essay as an opportunity to strut your hard-earned medals. Yet, recounting your accolades—however prestigious they may be--will not demonstrate what makes you tick. In other words, don't confuse what you do with who you are. More than your accomplishments, colleges want to know who you are.

The Writing Mindset

The first step in writing the college application essay is getting into the proper mindset. The right approach, it turns out, has less to do with what you achieve at work and more to do with who you are at play. Throw away your outline and allow yourself to write about what invigorates you.

Your essay is what distinguishes you from others who have similar GPAs, a plethora of extracurricular activities, and perfect test scores. The personal essay is the personification of you. How you portray yourself determines whether the admissions officer connects with you or not. Naturally, the admissions officer will be drawn more to essays that show depth of reflection, openness, and curiosity and less to ones that display boastfulness, intellectual hubris, and an inflated ego.

But old habits die hard, and it is difficult to suppress your desire to impress the admissions officer. When I told Sarah, my high achieving student who'd break out in hives at the mere mention of the words *college essay*, that she might approach the essay like an idler, she looked at me with the bemused, slightly uneasy air of a dog who is looking for the ball that his owner has only pretended to throw. "Uh…like relax, you mean?" Sarah asked, but in her eyes I read, "Seriously? I thought you were going to help me *write*!" Admittedly, Sarah had zero time to kick off her shoes and relax. She was the founding president of a charity organization, class president, and bent on getting a perfect 4.0. I assured her that somewhere behind all that frenzied activity, there was an amazing essay dying to get out—if only she'd sit still for a minute. Like so many others in her shoes, Sarah saw relaxation only as an escape from school duties.

After some days of fretful hand wringing, she handed me her first draft saying, "I know this is terribly boring, but it's all true." In sharp contrast to her considerable charm and wit, the essay was predictably a bore. It conveyed what I already knew to be the case with Sarah and so many other students like her: she was hard-working and accomplished. Clearly, she did not approach writing with joy, nor did she discover anything new about herself in the process of writing it. She wrote it as a matter of duty, a chore.

Sarah's trepidation about writing the personal essay is understandable given that she'd never written one before. Nothing in her high school English classes prepared her for writing to discover something new about herself. Mostly, she'd written argumentative or persuasive essays, relying on what she already knew. She'd begin with an outline, state her thesis, and provide supporting arguments in her body paragraphs. Like so many high school students, she was unprepared to boldly insert herself into the writing, to make herself the subject of inquiry.

Putting the draft aside, we began to talk about what she enjoyed doing. It was a long time since she had done anything out of sheer pleasure. Then she began to speak wistfully about her carefree 4-year-old sister, a trickster and a poet, who said things like, "When do trees ever sleep?" Through our conversation about her sister Abby, she came away with an essay topic about "serious play."

Like Sarah, I urge you to take a cue from little Abby and treat the college application essay as serious play. Lose yourself in the writing. Let's say, for instance, you want to write about your scuba-diving experience. Tell me what it feels like to listen underwater. What thoughts enter your mind? Describe the feel of a sea cucumber. Find out something about yourself that you did not know before. Reclaim the pleasure that comes with encountering a surprise. Now, share that gift of discovery with your reader through words. As with any worthwhile activity, if there is no happiness in the doing, your end product will be less than satisfactory.

I invite you to think about writing as a joyful practice. Think about what makes you tick. What gets you up in the morning? What makes you curious? In short, write about who you are, how you want to live, or how you want to revise your life.

Central to writing the personal essay is innovation. How do you say something new? On my shelf you will find books about the behavioral and neurological aspects of creativity; writers on writing; the science of motivation; the Zen of writing; the shape of a plot; and the artistic path of musicians, artists, and graphic designers. I synthesize insights from a wide array of disciplines and individuals to help you tap into your creativity. In writing this book, I am indebted to other writers, neurologists, graphic artists, painters, and musicians who have thought long and hard about how to communicate effectively and, in the process, produce works of art. In the spirit of collaboration and gratitude, I write this book to enable other writers like you. So relax and enjoy the ride. I always tell my students, "If you don't have fun writing it, then your reader will have no fun reading it."

In Part I, you will examine how you can prepare yourself for writing. You will learn techniques about how positive thinking and happiness, not anxiety, enhances your writing. You will learn how to glean inspiration from reading as you find out how to read like a writer. You will figure out how to walk around with your antennae picking up on every cue. You will see that there's inspiration even in a cat's meow if you're paying attention. You will discover that writing the personal essay is about making strange what is familiar and familiarizing what is strange.

The Personal Essay as Self-Discovery

In Part II, you will probe the nature of the personal essay. At its core, the personal essay is about self-discovery. Taking tips from some of the best essayists like Phillip Lopate, you will learn how to turn yourself into a character and tell an engaging story about that character. You will come to understand the anatomy of the personal essay. You will be introduced to various types of essays contained in the Common Application and college Supplements and, crucially, how to approach them. You will learn to interpret these prompts creatively as the first step toward delivering thought-provoking essays.

Crafting the Essay

In part III, you will learn about the distinct stages to writing. You will learn why you need to exercise divergent thinking when you are brainstorming and why revising is a little like interior decorating. You will learn how to recognize a good idea for a topic and crucially, how to develop that idea into your first draft. And you will learn how to get a bit of a distance from your essay when you craft your final version.

Tools for Writing

In Part IV, you will be introduced to the tools for writing. You will understand what it really means to show and not tell in your writing, why you should opt for the active voice, and how careful diction can help set the proper tone. You will master the art of writing with clarity and grace. In the final section, Part IV, you will study the collection of winning essays.

Why a Good Essay Tips the Scale

It is important to keep in mind that the essay is one part of the college application. You cannot underestimate or overestimate its weight in the review process. The essay will tip the scale in your favor only when all else is in place—your grades, standardized test scores, letters of recommendation, and extracurricular and volunteer work. In other words, I've never seen students get into their top choice college with a poor essay and I've never seen one admitted on a good essay alone. For highly competitive schools, however, the essay is what distinguishes you from the thousands of other students who have similar grades, test scores, and impressive accolades. A good essay gets you noticed. It reveals much about what motivates you, how you think, and why you are the way you are. Naturally, colleges favor someone who is innovative, sees himself or herself as part of a larger community, takes initiative, and values learning. In many instances, I have witnessed students with grade point averages below the threshold for the average admit gain admittance to their top choice college thanks to their superior essays. Since the personal essay is an ideal place for you to display these qualities, top tier colleges increasingly see the application essay as one of the most reliable measures of preparedness for college.

I believe that the essay will continue to play a significant role in determining the viability of candidates for admission. Recent studies like *Academically Adrift: Limited Learning on College Campuses* by Richard Arum and Josipa Roksa point to the rising number of college students who fail to demonstrate adequate writing skills. This problem makes students who are already talented writers all the more desirable to colleges.

CHAPTER One

Tilting Toward Happiness

"Happiness lies in the joy of achievement and the thrill of creative effort."—Franklin D. Roosevelt.

HERE IS A truism about bad writing: All bad writing emerges from unhappiness. But you might object, Franz Kafka was by all accounts not a particularly cheery person, and yet he was a magnificent writer! By unhappiness, then, I am not referring to one's disposition in life as much as one's orientation toward writing. I mean to say that good writing like that of Kafka emerges from the faith that the act of writing will uncover some hitherto unforeseen insight about life's conundrums. Unhappiness is the opposite of this faith: it is a lukewarm, resigned state of mind. Such unhappy orientation can never say anything new. Poor writing then arises out of a sense of duty. The unmotivated writer is its author. Even if structurally and grammatically sound, it is devoid of any emotive juice and a dimension of surprise. If you tackle the college admissions essay with as much enthusiasm as you might give over to cleaning the toilet, the only place for such wasted words is unfortunately down the drain.

What, then, is joy? And what does it have to do with writing? While it is commonly believed that writers are all depressed; as the neurologist Alice Flaherty points out, truly depressed people tend to write much less because depression renders everything meaningless. In fact, depression is said to be one of the biggest impediments to writing. It has a way of putting your life on hold. You have to approach writing in a positive state of mind, for your mood will help you to think outside the norm and uncover something new. When I was a child in Korea, I spent many a day stooped over, knee-deep in water, turning over stones. I was met with a string of surprises beneath the stones such as minnows, glistening mother of pearl, smooth pebbles, and salamanders. No words can describe the exhilaration that comes from discovering something new.

Ask any virtuoso and she will tell you that she loves what she does. This is not to say that what she does is easy. On the contrary, she will go through pain and great difficulty to achieve her goal, but this is only because she thoroughly enjoys her work. This joy and the devotion that spring from it are what fuel the virtuoso to produce something truly extraordinary. So it is with writing the personal essay. It takes both a wildness of imagination (that's the letting go part) and discipline. Don't write to be rewarded but find joy in the act of writing. Rely on an internal drive—what psychologists call *intrinsic motivation*. Forget that essay writing is about getting into college. Forget that getting into college is about succeeding (whatever that may mean to you). Free yourself from the fear of failing, disappointing your loved ones, or not measuring up to some yardstick that rewards or punishes. Let go of any guilt. And banish the nagging voice that says you can't do it. You've come this far, not because of some fluke but because you've earned it. You are going to write a knockout essay!

Once you've let go of all these deadening thoughts, it's just you and your blank screen or piece of paper. You are about to be engaged in what Sarah and I dubbed "serious play." Let's first get in the proper mood: tilt toward happiness. Listen to your favorite music. Take a long walk and try to notice the different bird sounds. Read something you love. Tune into your favorite comedy. Indulge in a warm shower. Studies have shown that you think well when you are happy and relaxed. The part of the brain activated by the punch line in a joke is the same part that lights up when you solve a particularly knotty problem. Jonah Lehrer, the author of *Imagine: How Creativity Works,* writes that eight seconds prior to the Aha! moment, you can predict through EEG (electroencephalogram) when you are about to have one. The precursory brain signal is an even rhythm of alpha waves originating from the right hemisphere. Scientists have long connected alpha waves with relaxing activities such as taking a warm shower or sleeping. Why is it critical to have a relaxed, joyful state of mind when doing creative work? When your mind is at ease, you are more able to direct your focus inward, making it possible to make remote and unusual associations. This is how insight happens. On the other hand, being too covetous of the prize (as in getting into your college of choice) creates a mental freeze; likewise, focusing on external details will prevent you from thinking outside-the-box. With a clenched mind, you will inhibit any creative connections and produce predictable writing.

Science amply demonstrates that there is a strong correlation between happiness and problem solving. In fact, people who score high on the standard measure of happiness are likely to score 25 percent higher on insight puzzles. The psychologist Alice Isen of Cornell University, a pioneer among researchers studying emotion and creativity, discovered that those subjects who were shown a five-minute clip of comedy as compared to those who watched a clip of a Nazi concentration camp and those who were shown nothing, performed far better at problem solving than either the Nazi-camp viewers or those shown nothing.

To maximize your potential for insight, try setting your alarm a little before your normal wakeup time. Neuroscientists point to early morning as the most optimal time for creative thinking. The brain that is half asleep is sufficiently unwound and radically open to all possibilities. I do my best thinking early in the morning. The germ for much of my writing comes to me before 6 a.m. Between sleep and waking, when dream streams into reality, anything can happen. A dog becomes werewolf. At this propitious hour, I reach for my pen and notebook and record the movie in my mind. This is often the most centering and joyful part of my day.

Lack of joy is one of the biggest contributors to writer's block. If you need to shake off some negative rumination, anxiety, or temporary melancholy, you might try the following top three solutions offered by Daniel Goleman in his book, *Emotional Intelligence,* for handling depression. Try aerobics exercise. Depression coincides with low arousal state and aerobics moves the body into high arousal. Try cognitive reframing; that is, consciously work on changing your perspective instead of wallowing in self-pitying thoughts. Reach out to someone else in need. While this last one may sound counterintuitive, studies have shown that empathizing allows you to focus on someone else's problems and, in the process; you give yourself an image boost.

There is a sadistic misconception out there that anything that's worth your effort is only gotten through blood, sweat, and tears. Gene Fowler famously said about writing: "All you have to do is sit staring at a blank sheet of paper until the drops of blood form on your forehead." His thinking is consonant with the age-old adage, "No pain, no gain!" This bedrock value in Western thought is as American as apple pie. Yet psychologists tell us the opposite is true. Granted writing is never easy, yet if I did not experience pleasure in writing, I would not do it. For me, there is no greater joy than being able to communicate effectively. Writing is the art of making a meaningful connection. It can be your way of saying, here I am, even though I am just one of 7 billion people on earth who were born and will die all the same. Still, against the backdrop of such an equalizing force as death, I yearn to share my unique discoveries in the journey between bookends.

No wonder most college application essays are uninspiring. For good, honest writing can never emerge from dread, fear, and anxiety. Such a negative mindset engenders stiff and pretentious writing. When you are relaxed and happy, you are better able to focus and make extra-ordinary associations. So when you are facing the blank screen or the white paper, begin by letting go. Let go of all self-doubt. Enjoy the delicious feeling of going on a ride to who knows where. Greet the page as though it were a welcome mat.

Happiness will help secure the most essential quality in your essay. But how do you go about invoking creativity? Wouldn't it be just amazing to turn it on whenever you wanted it? Mihaly Csikszentmihalyi, the premier psychologist of creativity, thinks that you can do that by trying to understand how creativity works. He states that creative individuals tend toward *complexity*. Like the color white containing all the colors of the rainbow, they "bring together the entire range of human possibilities within themselves." They are paradoxically capable of entertaining, for example, two opposing points of view at the same time without much difficulty. The creative individual is like the protagonist in *The Woman Warrior* by Maxine Hong Kingston, who says regarding the clash of Chinese and Western cultures, "I tried to make my mind large, as large as the universe is large, so that there is room for paradoxes."

This ability to make unusual, seemingly contradictory connections is the defining characteristic of a good essay. You can get there with good intuition and judgment. Intuition is what attunes you to what is not yet; it is what launches you into taking that leap of imagination. With good judgment, you will know exactly when to launch into the improbable and when to wed yourself to what is in front of your nose. One of my students, Jason, wanted to write about an object that changed his life. He chose to write about the alarm clock his mother gave him before she passed away. He writes concerning the clock, "Over the years it has become for me, a clarion call from my mother, a personal wake up call. The word alarm comes from an old Italian phrase *all'arme* which means to arms! It is a call to arm myself against a possible attack. While I hardly think that my days are literal battlefields, there is a sense in which I have to mentally equip myself to face the challenges as well as opportunities put before me every day. That means persevering through the roughest storms."

The moment of discovery happened when Jason came to see the clock as a reminder that he should not only work hard but also be happy. This realization enabled him to get past his own depression. In the concluding lines of his essay, Jason wrote, "I've begun to set the alarm to my favorite radio station. In addition to being mentally prepared for my daily challenges, I think my mother would have wanted me to start my day on a happy note."

This brings to mind my next point. Creative individuals also embrace a combination of playfulness and discipline. Colton was just such a student. In his sophomore year, he led his team to win the creativity title in the world championship of the Odyssey of the Mind. And his early admission to Yale University was a testament to his unstoppable drive. In the following tale, Colton demonstrates how he used his creativity and tenacity not only to help him succeed academically but also to assist him in fulfilling the wish of a special friend. "My friend has suffered more than what most people will ever know…. It has been heartbreaking to watch him slowly lose his good humor and optimism…. It is my duty as a friend to do whatever I can to fulfill his (Nachu Bhatnager's) last wishes," writes Colton in an open letter on Reddit.org. His long-time friend, left with only six months to live, had mentioned in passing his one re-gret—that he would not live to read the last installment of Harry Turtledove's series *The War That Came Too Early.* Committed to making his friend's wish come true, Colton brushed aside his mounting homework and put out a query on the Internet about how he might attain an editor's copy of the book for his friend. Moved by Colton's plea, responses started pouring in. So and so knew the daughter of the author, and another knew his editor. By 2 a.m. he had secured a copy of the book. And by the week-end, he was on the plane to deliver the book to his friend. You can watch the moving interchange here http://www.hlntv.com/article/2012/02/28/reddit-helps-man-cancer-harry-turtledove-book. This heart-warming tale about a friendship also turns out to be a story about how Colton acted on a whim and delivered on a promise, despite improbable odds that he would obtain it. Anyone who reads this story will see that creative people with discipline possess a powerful combination for success. If you practice living creatively, you will write highly engaging essays.

CHAPTER **TWO**

Reading to Write

"Reading is the sole means by which we slip, involuntarily, often helplessly, into another's skin, another's voice, another's soul."—Joyce Carol Oats

TO UNDERSCORE THE active engagement required in reading, the writer and philosopher Sartre cautioned against lying down when reading. Reading is indispensable for the writer. Trying to write without reading is like trying to play the cello without listening to Yo Yo Ma. In observing the greats, you perfect your own technique and learn what has been done before and how you might contribute in unique ways. In sixth grade, I had my first taste of how it feels to put words down on a page. Mrs. Mellor, my favorite English teacher wielding a contagious smile and a bounce in her step, doled out poems like they were candy. Preparing to read, she'd close the blinds and wait for us to settle until you could hear a pin drop. I still hear her voice echo in my mind as I read the poems she first read to me. When she read Edgar Allen Poe's *The Raven*, I was stirred to try my hand at writing a poem myself. Perhaps it was the musical repetition of the refrain, "quoth the Raven, `Nevermore'" that moved me to imitate its rhythm. I loved turning over words, playing with line breaks, and weighing the sound and sense of words to try and convey the meaning I intended. "Words are like freight trains," she'd tell us, "make sure they carry the meaning you intend." I cannot remember what it was I wrote, only that it was a poem about freedom and that it pleased Mrs. Mellor. I was happy to see the words line up to approximate what I felt inside. Reading it out loud in front of my class, I felt immense pleasure in being able to create with words.

In this age of quick sound bites, texting, and infinite access to information at our fingertips, too many temptations stand in the way of reading and writing. A study of 2,500 students showed that they spent a bit over 3 hours a day Facebooking, surfing the Internet, and texting.

Richard Arum and Josipa Roksa, referencing this study, conclude that diminished reading time--as more time is spent on the Internet--correlates with poor writing.

Consider the humble black type set against a white page as compared to the plethora of alluring digitized applications put before us. The bookworm has taken a bite out of the iconic Apple and the screen has replaced the printed page. Without fostering a habit of reading, it is difficult to become creative, critical thinkers and writers. I've seen students who don't read bring home straight A's but fail to write effectively.

Neuroscience tells us that reading transforms the everyday journey into an epic voyage. Stories can change how we act. Scientists, observing what happens to the brain when we read, demonstrate that a good read allows us to relive what is written on paper. When I was a little girl, I remember Gene, the host on a Saturday morning art show. He would draw characters that would literally walk off the pages. From freshly drawn characters the stories unfurled. Good writing, too, has that ability to stimulate that part of the brain to bring you into the story with all your senses and motor skills. Neuroscience confirms what the reader already knows: that the phrase, "the guitar player made a pleasant sound," doesn't move as much as "the guitar player unraveled the knot in my heart." When you read "the trumpet green Eucalyptus," the sensory cortex--distinct from the language processing part of the brain--will light up as though you had came upon it yourself. Likewise, if you read, "the old man shuffled across the street unmindful of the traffic light blinking yellow" your motor cortex will light up as though you were right there at the street corner.

Reading makes you smarter. The brain is not a fixed entity. Like a muscle, you can exercise it into shape. Reading makes your mind suppler. It enables you to become creative in problem solving, increase memory function, focus better, and reason more effectively. And when you make reading a life-long habit, it can help stave off mental illness and dementia to boot. It has been known to increase memory and listening skills. With overall improvements in cognition, reading is the answer to becoming better learners.

Reading also teaches empathy. Since stories allow you to get inside people's heads, it allows you to better understand what motivates and triggers certain emotions and moods in people. Stories help to unravel complex social situations and the web of relations that inform worldviews and behaviors. Being able to walk in someone else's shoes helps you to better understand yourself and others. To illustrate, Jonathan Franzen in his essay, "My Father's Brain," memorably describes what I've come to see as the stiff-lipped mid- western persona: "My father had always been supremely suspicious of psychiatry. He viewed therapy as an invasion of privacy, mental health as a matter of self-discipline, and my mother's increasingly pointed suggestion that he "talk to someone" as acts of aggression—little lobbed grenades of blame for their unhappiness as a couple." That metaphor—"little lobbed grenades of blame"—is a clincher! Reading this essay gave me greater clarity and compassion toward persons I know who remind me of Franzen's father. In short, reading increases your emotional intelligence, which, according to the fore-mentioned psychologist Goleman, impacts every decision you make from choosing your college major to your life partner. Reading can enrich your life.

It also attunes your mind to pay attention. You become a keen observer of life. When you read, you enter into a new place. A book turns every reader into a traveler. In traveling you insert yourself into an unfamiliar setting. On my first trip to Sicily, beneath the canopy of oleander trees I looked out at the sea still frisky after the storm and I became a character in a play with no script. Strolling down the tree-lined promenade bathed in that peculiar amber light as intoxicated as a blind person gaining sight for the first time, I was overcome by the peach-colored oleander blossoms. Reading attunes your mind to look at things anew.

Reading inspires. Inspiration is your creative muse that jumpstarts your voice to speak or write. Put differently, it is the "undertow" in writing. Upon returning from a trip to the Pacific coast with tides fresh on my mind, I began to think about the undertow as a metaphor for inspiration. The undertow tugs me in. I have to lean into it rather than resist by trying to take control. When you inspire, you take in something unfamiliar. This tussling with the strange is crucial to the creative process. Without inspiration, you have no voice. When writers talk about finding their voice, I used to imagine a ventriloquist dummy suddenly being loosed to speak on its own. I thought that voice, once found, ran constantly like an open spigot. Little did I know that without a constant infusion of inspiration, the inner voice dries up. So I read unceasingly seeking inspiration—that encounter with something outside myself that awakens my own voice to speak.

In seeking inspiration, you are trying to understand better who you are and what you should do with your life. But to grow, you must take in the world. Eat, digest, and grow into someone larger than who you are now. Iris Murdoch, the novelist and philosopher once said, "Love is the very difficult understanding that something other than yourself is real." In the process of mulling over the reality of what is not familiar, you learn to acknowledge the inspiration meant to help you grow. Reading awakens my own desire to create something beautiful. Like an inspired chef, once I've tasted something worth repeating, I am moved to make it myself. Each morsel keeps me guessing. *Was that a hint of nutmeg in the squash ravioli?* One of my favorites is a pear dessert I uncovered in a little known Florentine *trattoria*. Pears are more intriguing than their cousin apples, for they ripen from the inside out. This is a good metaphor for inspiration. Give it time and it will mature from within and make itself known through writing. Poached in red wine and spiced with orange peels, anise star, cardamom, and cinnamon sticks, there is no winter dessert more royal than this globed goodness sitting in a sweet Burgundy sap. Biting into one of these will transform you. Poaching—continuing with the metaphor--is akin to the crystallization of words into art. A naked pear in the end is transformed into something much larger than itself. Its complex flavors, form, and texture deliver an irresistible experience. It tastes decidedly strange and yet familiar. This is how it feels to be inspired. Your voice becomes inflected as it grapples with something surprising outside yourself when you read a good book.

Just as a connoisseur of fine dining might find herself bent over a hot stove concocting a delectable wine sauce, the avid reader eventually turns out masterpieces herself. Reading, like nothing else, fires my desire to write. By reading, you develop an instinct and an ear for what clicks and connects powerfully with your audience.

CHAPTER **Three**

Put up your Antennae

*"Life is all memory, except for the one present moment
that goes by you so quickly you hardly catch it going."*
–Tennessee Williams

WRITERS WALK THROUGH life as though entering a cave with
a strobe light fastened to their foreheads. Equipped with a cen-
trifugal vortex that sucks up everything in their path, writers
cause a minor whirlwind when they pass by. They are attentive, not discriminating. The world is one big possibility full of
knick-knacks and all things esoteric. When you are on the path,
you might not know exactly what you are looking for, but you
will know when you see it. Serendipity is the happy accident
of finding something you didn't expect to find. There are days
when I get up in the morning delighted at the thought of finding
some surprise around the corner. One such morning, I'd found
on my walk August bush poppies, a bed of catmint, low creep-
ing thyme, mossy burls, slug trails, and robins under a patch of
light for the morning feed. Back in my kitchen, I sat for hours
with my pen and paper over my breakfast tea writing a personal
essay for my newly found treasure. I like entering into this zone.
Present. Open. Attentive. Ready to be surprised.

Your inspiration will come when you least expect it. This is a tale about how Melinda stumbled upon an essay topic. As she pulled into the turning lane and gave her signal to drive up the park ramp, a turkey abruptly strutted out into the crosswalk as though he were just another pedestrian. Melinda remembers thinking how she wouldn't have been surprised if he toted a briefcase. Upon a closer look, however, she noticed how comically disheveled he looked with a loose feather hanging from his chest. He reminded her of a man she once saw in a suit and tie, waving down a bus, looking businesslike except for his off-kilter toupee flapping in the wind. The turkey went first this way, then that, keeping her, along with now a long line of cars queuing up behind her, from turning. Melinda saw something of herself in the lost bird: "In movement, I become disassociated with my moving body. My brain recedes from me, unable, as it were, to deliver to my consciousness my orientation at any given moment. The resulting disorientation can be attributed to a neurological processing dysfunction that lags and unmoors me." As the image of the lost turkey insinuated itself onto her mental landscape, she found herself writing for some days about the times she got lost. That is how she came to write about her lack of direction. The twist in the essay came when she reflected on how her "dance with the world assumed an ongoing negotiation of leading and letting go, of missteps and somersaults." Whether you are on a walk, going through your family album, recounting your dreams, reading a book, or watching a movie, put up your antennae. You never know when a lost turkey will speak to you as it did to Melinda.

Write What You See

"Vision is the art of seeing what is invisible to others." – Jonathan Swift

WRITING MANIFESTS A new way of seeing. Seeing is not merely recording. By seeing, I mean paying witness to something as yet unseen. In seeing you are uncovering something true, and according to historian Caroline Bynum, truth is decidedly strange. As a reminder to herself that wonder more than facts inspires the story teller, she has above her desk this epithet: "Every view of things that is not strange is false" (a Paris wall slogan from the student rebellion of 1968). Annie Dillard, the award-winning essayist, in her piece "Seeing" reflects on her formative years growing up in the backwoods of Pittsburgh. Writing, for Dillard, "is a matter of keeping [her] eyes open." She encourages seeing as if seeing for the first time. For the newly sighted, she explains, vision is pure sensation unencumbered by meaning. She describes one such newly sighted who saw nothing "but a lot of different kinds of brightness" and another who saw "nothing but a confusion of forms and colors." Stephen Kuuisto, the poet born with retinopathy, saw colors and torn geometries. Describing a walk to the end of a jetty with his father in Helsinki, Finland, he saw no distinctions between sky and ice, only the endless plain of gray Baltic light. A troop of singing women would emerge from the mist and just as mysteriously disappear into the black and green liquid. In the mind's eye of the artist, what he saw through his purblind vision unhinged a desire to travel and see the world despite his blindness. You can get a taste of his poetic prose in his memoir *Eavesdropping*.

Sophie reflects on how *seeing* involves imagining beyond what meets the eye. In an essay using Shel Silverstein's *Where the Sidewalk Ends* as inspiration, Sophie contemplates how imagination and science though seemingly at odds with one another, in fact, go hand-in-hand. She writes, "The sidewalk ends at the edge of reality, where the last jagged piece of gray cement juts out over a purple mantel of possibilities. Here the harsh lines of reality blur and bleed together with imagination; the façade is stripped away to unveil the truth." Distinctive is her vivid detailing of the space that defines her reality. Metaphorically speaking, she juxtaposes the "jagged pieces of cement" with "purple mantels" to signify the difference between reality and imagination. Seeing the truth, for Sophie, depends on stripping away at the "façade" to get at the truth.

As Sophie demonstrates, seeing is not a mere record of an event but an insightful detailing of competing realities. As the saying goes, god is in the details. No one goes through life generally. No one is an abstraction. It matters that on that afternoon after the funeral you sat across from Aunt Dolores drinking chocolate malt, staring blankly at the vintage banner of the Barnum and Bailey Circus. Just as each person has a unique genetic signature, you give expression to your singularity through words. Writing is a way of saying yes to everything that matters to you despite or perhaps—depending on how you look at it—in light of our mortality. Thus, details redeem life. Without details, there would be nothing more to the human story than that we are born, we live, and then we die. Yet ever since humans could hold the brush or the pen, we have been telling the richly detailed stories of our lives on stone tablets, cave walls, eggshells, parchment, or paper.

However keen your sight and insight, all the noticing in the world is not going to turn you into a writer unless you write down what you notice. Writing down what you see is a form of drawing attention to the act of observing. John Rushkin, a nineteenth-century English art critic and essayist says that without writing it down, it is "not merely unnoticed, but in the full, clear sense of the word, unseen." In a given day, the average human has 70,000 thoughts. Without a record, your ideas are here one moment and gone the next.

A notebook is a must in every writer's toolkit. A notebook, journal, or a diary—call it what you will—should be by your side. I have one by my bedside, one in my purse, and another in my kitchen. I even carry one in my gym bag. When I am reading a book or hiking in the woods, my notebook and pen is within reach. I never buy a notebook too fancy or expensive since for one, I go through them so quickly; and secondly, I might feel obligated to say something too precious. In fact, my notebook is far from being decorous; it is more like that miscellaneous drawer in the kitchen filled with batteries, scraps of paper, matches, scissors, old grocery lists, toothpicks, used birthday candles, pens, and pennies. In my notebook, I record snippets of memories, new words, old words used in new ways, grocery lists, etchings of a poem, recipes, notes for a short piece of fiction or essays, dreams, sketches, titles of books and films, and free writes. If I had not written down my impression of that blind man I saw on the train, I might not remember how he wore mismatched socks and sat reading his braille book with such a blissful expression.

In her notebook, Jamie, another student of mine, came across the phrase "shoes on electric wires" that prompted the beginning lines of an essay that starts with "A humble pair made with a guileless, white canvass, rubbery soles, and a pair of reedy lace." Her essay, which she titled, "Hope Dangling on Wire" turned out to be a reflection about the imagined shoe-thrower who'd come out in the middle of the night to hang his hopes on a blinkered world. Another one of my students Taylor shared that he carries around little strips of paper like the ones inside fortune cookies. The strips force him to compress his thoughts into a word or a phrase, and at the end of the day he drops them into a box the way one might throw coins into a piggy bank.

Practice Makes Perfect

"Being a professional is doing the things you love to do on the days you don't feel like doing them." –Julius Erving

WHAT DO BASKETBALL players and writers have in common? Julius Erving will tell you that it's all in the practice! I wish I could tell you that there was some magic formula for instantly turning out immaculate essays over night. There isn't. You have to give yourself at least the summer before your senior year to develop the practice of writing. Yet some of you may not be convinced that practice has anything to do with writing well. You may harbor the mindset that there are writers--more or less born with the talent--and there are non-writers—those who can't write no matter how hard they try. This is false. It turns out that your beliefs about intelligence or raw talent have much to do with your own motivation for mastering writing. Take this little quiz. Fill in the equation: Intelligence = __ % ability + __ % effort. According to Carol Dweck, psychologist and author of *Mindset,* if you hold an *entity theory* of intelligence, then you give more weight to innate ability. If you adhere to an *incremental theory* of intelligence, then you are likely to believe that your brain is like a muscle that can be exercised to grow.

Depending on your mindset, you can choose to look smart or actually challenge yourself to learn something new; you can be motivated merely to put on a good performance or alternatively, attain mastery; in the face of criticism, you can believe you are dumb or resolve to learn from the experience. Numerous studies show that incremental mindset on intelligence is highly effective for meeting your challenges and building greater resilience. So start the practice of writing today!

Aristotle, the famous ancient Greek philosopher once wrote, "We are what we repeatedly do. Excellence, then, is not an act, but a habit." As Malcolm Gladwell explains in his book *Outliers: the Story of Success,* the Beatles, learned to improve their technique when they were booked for 8 hour-long show times in Hamburg. Pete Best, the then drummer of the Beatles explained, "We played seven nights a week. At first we played almost nonstop till twelve-thirty, when it closed, but as we got better the crowds stayed till two most mornings." In less than a month, they played over 170 hours on stage. Gladwell introduces the 10, 000 hour-rule, the pre-requisite number of hours of practice needed to attain mastery whether playing basketball or programming computers. While he acknowledges innate talent, he argues that without putting in the hours mastery cannot be achieved. So it is with writing. You can become an expert if you work at it everyday. Make it a goal to write everyday, starting out with half an hour commitment daily.

What Is the Personal Essay?

"Every man has within himself the entire human condition."—Michel de Montaigne

AT THE HEART of the essay is experimentation. It is like taking a path not known. My friend once told me that her best hiking experience happened when she went off trail to follow a deer path. It brought her to a family of deer by a small pond. When you are writing your essay, throw away your outline. They are as useless as maps when there are no signposts. You are writing to discover something new; your conclusion can never be in hand. This is what makes writing the personal essay exciting and scary.

On a hot day in August, I took my daughter on a wild goose chase on Bus # 25 to the outskirts of Bologna, Italy in search of an organic outdoor market. A quintessential adventure for me is hopping on a bus to a place I've never been, preferably in a foreign country, relying on perfect strangers to get me there. I recall the misguided directions, the wrong turns, not to mention the dangerous shoulder of a freeway. "And all that," my daughter complained, "for a bag of wilted spinach!" While she rolled her eyes and said how it was a miracle that I was still alive, she couldn't help but laugh. We laughed our hearts out on that narrow road to market with the sunflower field to our left and speeding cars to our right. And there are days when my daughter and I are kicking dirt on a road to god knows where, but I'm always asking, "What's it all about?" Were I to develop this story about my expedition into a personal essay, I would write that more than the bag of wilted spinach I was in search of something more fundamental, connected to my desire to find something out of the ordinary. The surprise for me was discovering a reversal of roles: my daughter home from college playing the parent, and I, the reckless one, striking out toward the unknown.

As a mixed genre—part fiction and part nonfiction—the personal essay is a story about the "I" *plus* reflection. You don't need to write a personal essay if your main point is that you worked hard for your achievements. For the fact remains that just about everyone applying to colleges is hard-working. To reference your industriousness is to beat a dead horse. Instead, take a random bus ride and tell a story about a time you learned something about yourself that you had not known before. The very desire to make sense of your life is what makes for an engaging tale.

Here is another way to think about the personal essay. Real life often offers no plausible plot; you write to find order. In the muck of your everyday existence, you move from one event to the next with little thread of continuity or meaning. There are days that feel to be long digressions. The personal essay allows you to bring coherence, significance, and meaning to those seemingly disconnected events. It brings order amid chaos. Gustave Flaubert writes, "Human speech is like a cracked kettle on which we tap crude rhythms for bears to dance to, while longing to make music to melt the stars." Write a story about yourself as if your life's very meaning depends on it.

Key Features of the Personal Essay

"A writer is someone for whom writing is more difficult than it is for others." –Thomas Mann

RESONANCE

The chief mission of the personal essayist is to "resonate" with the reader. Whenever I give a workshop on writing, I take a little bell along to demonstrate this key feature in writing. From the Latin root meaning to resound, resonate means "to produce or be filled with a deep, reverberating sound." When you strike a note, you are hitting a chord that touches your reader. In this way, your reader is moved by your words. This give and take between the writer and the reader is like an intimate conversation. The act of writing then deepens the common ground in humanity by rendering a private matter into a public one.

HONESTY

Intimacy between the writer and reader is established when the writer is honest. James Baldwin, the essayist and the author of "Notes of a Native Son" writes, "I want to be an honest man and a good writer." Baldwin understands that without honesty good writing does not happen. A lie, then, is a mask, a guard put up to prevent true engagement with the reader. Yet telling the truth is so hard to maintain. To lie is to be human. For we want to hide all the ways in which we see ourselves as blemished and imperfect people. Phillip Lopate, the personal essayist explains, "The plot in the personal essay on some level is about seeing how far the author can go in being honest." A good piece of writing, then, exposes some aspect of the author's vulnerability. The decorous, self-assured, organization man in suit and tie will not likely become a good personal essayist. In fiction or in real life, people are drawn to honesty.

VULNERABILITY

Honesty is a prerequisite for risking vulnerability. When writing the personal essay, the first mistake beginning writers make is to write something they think the admissions officers want to hear. They think that their lives are unremarkable. Playing it safe, they write a trite essay about the perfect high school senior who is disciplined, smart, and high achieving. They say nothing to distinguish themselves from others who write variations on the same. They mean to impress but they more often bore or worse, turn off the admissions officer. Consider this self-aggrandizing statement from a student: "After a rewarding year of hard work and impact, accepting that beautiful, first place plaque at the FBLA National Leadership Conference was priceless. That plaque represented for me the smiling faces of my team, optimistic nods of the community, and personal satisfaction." I conveyed to this student that statements like this give the impression that she is smug, self-satisfied, and seemingly unperturbed by anything. Motivated to seek praise and acceptance, ego-driven writers create portraits of near perfection. I explained that making oneself vulnerable takes courage. In time the student came to revise this passage to: "Our efforts to bring awareness about the green house effect earned us recognition at the FBLA National Leadership Conference. Our recognition, in turn, further sparked the green awareness campaign from the far reaches of Florida to California."

CURIOSITY

The proper psychological stance for the personal essayist is curiosity. Lopate suggests that turning yourself into a character is the best way to achieve this state of self-curiosity. Get a little distance by imagining yourself as a character. Like Dickens's ghost of Christmas, try to see yourself in a movie. Step outside of yourself and observe as though you were drawing a portrait of yourself. Or, look at yourself in the mirror and try to describe yourself as others might see you. Are you funny, driven, tired, or anxious? Or do you aspire to become something you are not as yet?

Story Is Key

At the center of the essay is the story. A story is different from a narrative. A narrative is just a series of neutral statements. A story has movement, plot, suspense, scene description, character development, conflict, and resolution. Placing yourself in a story means that you are changed in the process of doing something. Do you know how powerful a good story can be? According to Daniel Pink, the author of *A Whole New Mind,* economists calculate a good persuasive story--be it in advertising, counseling, consulting, or writing—to account for 25 percent of U.S. gross domestic product. Story, being central to all these efforts, then, is worth about $1 trillion a year to the U.S. economy. Learning how to write a good story will reap benefits beyond getting into the college of your choice.

Whatever else might be said about a story, it has to hold interest. It is the inflected voice of the narrator that drives the story. Consider these two sentences: *Sergeant McDonnell was killed in the Iraqi war. His mother died shortly thereafter.* Now see what happens when you link the two sentences: *Upon hearing the news of her son's death in the Iraqi war, Mrs. McDonnell died of a broken heart.* Notice how the second example creates interest by establishing causality between the soldier's death and that of the mother. By linking A to B, you weave a story and in the process provide meaning to what may appear merely coincidental.

Tone and Voice

The tone is your attitude toward the subject at hand. In the college application essay whatever tone you take up, you must deliver an intimate feel much like a personal letter. To help you set the proper tone, think of the admissions officer as your aunt come to dinner to give you undivided attention. Voice is a little more involved: it is how you come off to your reader. You will want to sound open, humorous, curious, and sympathetic rather than dogmatic, inflexible, and closed-minded. It is that intangible quality your reader will pick up right away. Voice, I once explained in my writing workshop, is what makes you drop everything and listen. It is a merging of the familiar with the strange. I told the story of my newly-born daughter, lying in the tiny crib crying her lungs out. Too weak to walk, I called out her name. To my amazement, she ceased her crying and turned her head my way. What notions could this neo-natal upon hearing my voice entertain? Perhaps she found some comfort there. But by the look on her face, I think it also took her by surprise, for my voice piqued her curiosity even as it struck a chord of familiarity.

CHAPTER Seven

The Shape of the Personal Essay

"By applying cunning…you fashion the ordered world of a story." –Peter Selgin

WHILE NO SINGULAR template exists for how you begin or end a personal essay, I can give some examples for creating a shapely essay. By using the same tools necessary for writing good fiction and through carefully chosen diction, you can achieve an artful essay. A common tendency among beginning writers is to attempt to tell too much. Think of a small sliver of your life. "By focusing on a single button," advised my writing mentor once, "you can reconstitute an entire suit."

First, a word on beginnings. Your first sentence is arguably the most salient sentence. It is what introduces you to the reader. It sets the tone, introduces your voice, and provides a clue about the topic at hand. Moreover, a good beginning sentence creates intrigue or mystery to whet your reader's appetite. I had an editor once tell me that whether he continues to read or not is contingent upon the first sentence. In so many words, you have to hook your reader. Here are some winning first liners from my former students. Try and see why they work. What do you notice regarding the connection between diction, tone, and voice? From these lines, do you expect to hear something out of the ordinary?

I fell in love with history in the back seat of my dad's 1967 blue Chevrolet.

It is a wonder, really, what I can do with a pair of hands.

The sidewalk ends at the edge of reality, where the last jagged piece of gray cement juts out over a purple mantel of possibilities.

Freshman year brought extremes to my sense of touch.

Jealous of my brother who participated in Little League baseball, I asked my parents if I too could have a trophy.

My mother used to tell me that she could stick her fingernail into the walls of my grandparent's house and the dust from the plaster would come crumbling down.

Gazing out the car window, she asked, "When do trees sleep? They are always standing."

My trip to Mexico followed me around like a shadow, arms akimbo, and poking me, saying—"Do something!"

I flick on the light switch, illuminating what must surely be the most baffling garage in Moraga.

Now that you have your reader's attention, you can jump right in to tell your story. Take us right to the middle and zoom

MASTERING THE COLLEGE APPLICATION ESSAY

in on the scene. You don't have to start at the beginning. Take us to the action. I am going to use Lyon's scouting essay to demonstrate the shape of an essay. He begins with these lines that sets the stage for his adventure. *As the sun burns through the fog, my fellow comrades and I trudge through chest deep mud, beleaguered and fatigued.* Lyon wastes no time parachuting his reader smack in the middle of the trenches. With colorful diction, he develops the opening scene and helps his reader to get into the mood of the story. In the next couple of sentences, he introduces himself as the main character in the story carrying a heavy canoe. *The weight of the eighty-pound canoe upon my shoulders sends waves of muscle pinching pain. Upon the eleventh hour patience become myth, and every sinew in my body focuses on the finish line.* We can identify with the formidable journey put before him. The language remains highly visual.

In the next segment, the writer zooms out and gives us the broader context so that we can situate the story. *This is Northern Tier country, forty minutes outside of Bissett, Canada, a place scouts have come to call Heartbreak. Northern Tier offers breathtaking views of crystal lakes and eternally green treetops. With beauty comes a price, however, and before a scout may reach salvation, he must encounter his final test, one of the toughest terrains known to mankind. I've come from a world that has little remorse for those who are not prepared, and scouting has shaped my life to always expect the unexpected.* In the last line, he presents what sounds like a thesis. Most personal essays in fact don't have a thesis, but Lyon puts one out there without sounding too heavy handed.

Lyon develops the story further and, crucially, begins to weave in his reflection. *Northern Tier provided me a bubble, isolated from the world. Every motion, every movement, and every decision had a consequence, and whether the effect was positive or negative, it was exigent and real. When everything you do directly influences your next move, a new sense of clarity arises, and every detail receives an unparalleled focus.* Then he resumes the story building up tension as the plot unfolds. *On our eighth day, with every muscle trembling with exhaustion, I reached the last portage before Beaver Damnation.*

As the lake came into view, I replayed the fantasy over and over again in my mind of that cathartic dropping of the canoe. Now, left or right? If I drop to my right a rock could pierce the hull of our canoe and doom us all. If I go left, a massive leech will gain an opportunity to squelch up my pant leg and latch on to my calf. The canoe's weight was unbearable. I had to choose quickly. A fellow scout yells something in my ear. Suddenly I realize I'm falling. Time's up! Feeling my body engulfed by the brisk water, I knew I had made the right choice. By now the reader is thoroughly invested as the plot thickens and is relieved to know that he has made the right choice. There is comic relief in the end with a leech attack. *As we paddled across Sasiginnigak Lake, I relished the thought of having saved the day. That is, until I felt a burning pain on my shin. I hate leeches.* A sense of humor is always welcome!

In the ensuing section, Lyon concludes by deepening his reflection. Notably, he does not harp on what is by now a cliché college application theme of responsibility, teamwork, or leadership. Moreover, note how he never says outright that he is reliable, persistent, responsible, or prudent. But by telling an engaging story, he amply demonstrates that he possesses all these qualities and more. What he does choose to tell in the aftermath of the story is far more subtle and sophisticated: *Every day we are plagued with insignificance. We go on autopilot and make decisions with little consequence or care. Our routines numb us to boredom. We fail to be captured by what is in front of us. My experience at Northern Tier made me realize in ret-rospect that I can't afford to cruise through life. Like paint to canvas, Northern Tier awakened me to a more vibrant life. Years of scouting have taught me about perseverance and presence of mind. With these lessons, I hope to further shape my life to become a man with the heart of a scout.*

Finally, let's reflect on endings. Lyon brings the story full circle by reminding his readers where it all began—in Northern Tier. He reiterates the lesson learned by using a refreshing anal-ogy; and by referencing "the heart of a scout," Lyon ends on a fitting and a light-hearted note.

You will want to avoid the over-the-top endings typical of college application essays. You know the kind I mean. For ex-ample, it would seem over-reaching to write that your helping to build a house for a poor family in Tijuana for a week motivates you to dedicate your life to eradicating poverty. Statements like that make you sound overly naïve. You might choose to end with a quote or a dialogue. Here is an ending from a student who wrote about being left-handed. *So in my various decisions and roads ahead of me, I might go the left way instead of the right way, but at last I would leave behind footprints in the road less traveled. And that makes all the difference.* Cogent but play-ful, her last lines remain true to the winsome tone of her essay. Lastly, here is an ending about the process of art-making. *While it would be easy for me to hide, I step out despite my fears knowing and remembering the exhilaration of finding out some-thing I had not known about myself and feeling suddenly the world drawing a little closer to me.* In this concluding statement, the author is hinting at a change in perspective not a blueprint for her future.

Interpreting Essay Prompts

AS YOU PLAN your essays, it might help you to think about your application as a balanced meal. That is, all your essays should coalesce to forge a whole picture of yourself. Demonstrate through your writing that you are not only intellectually curious but also deeply committed to social change. For instance, as an aspiring engineer, your essays should show your penchant for designing medical equipment along with your leadership in the juvenile rehabilitation center. Similarly, as a pre-law student, just one essay will do on your love of debating and the remainder of your essays should focus on how your love of gardening turned into a project that collects and delivers fresh produce to the local food pantry. Likewise, if you incline towards computer science, play up your lighter, humanist side and make sure that some of your responses deal with your inclination for drawing, passion for working with Alzheimer patients, or your love of the violinist Itzhak Perlman.

To flesh out your self-portrait, you will want to use every opportunity from one-liners to long essays to put your best self forward. There are long essays (with a maximum word-count of 650) and short answers in the supplements (ranging from just a couple of lines to 250 words). Depending on the school, you may have to submit as little as 3 responses or as many as 10. As you write your replies, here are some common myths to keep in mind about the college essay prompts:

> *Myth # 1: As long as your main Common Application essay remains artful, you will not be penalized for less than stellar answers to the short essay prompts. Your job is to provide more or less straightforward replies to the short essay prompts.*

This statement could not be farther from the truth. All your responses should be delivered with equal degree of attention and care. When the admissions officers see inconsistencies in the writing between the main essay and the short answers, they will assume that someone else may have authored the more polished essay. As my student David demonstrates, the short answers can be written artfully. This is his reply to the prompt: *Tell us about an activity that is particularly meaningful to you. "Freshman year brought extremes to my sense of touch. The bruises I sustained playing football could tell you. And yet after all the collisions between flesh, the beautiful arc of gyrating leather, the rallying yells, the raw feeling of the hunt, I went home to help take care of my one-year-old sister. She liked to wrap her hand around my pinky. I slipped into both roles gracefully, and into far more too. I was a football player, a brother, a son, a scholar, an engineer, a manager, a musician, and a citizen. In my book of hours, I am touched by these and much more and feel blessed that in response I can viciously tackle and gingerly hug."*
There are times, as in this case, when your response can subtly interrogate the very premise of the prompt, by exposing

its oversimplification. Anthony's reply questions whether one can be defined by a singular activity. For him, it is the juxtaposition of what would appear to be extreme types of activities that define him.

Myth # 2: The key to writing great essays is coming up with highly unusual topics.

Not necessarily. I've seen some great essays on one-of-a-kind topics such as finger-painting on frosted windows, left-handedness, and spatial dyslexia, but such run-of-the-mill subjects like being a boy scout, a soccer player, or a runner have also produced amazing essays. Good writing lies not as much in the *what* as in the *how*. When admissions officers are reading your essays, they are interested in the *lens* through which you view your experiences.

Myth # 3: It is a waste of your time to start writing before the prompts have been officially announced which typically happens in late summer.

This statement is false. Think about the plodding turtle that wins the race as opposed to the overly confident hare that, upon waking from his nap, attempts to make a mad dash for the finish line. Starting early is especially crucial when it comes to writing college application essays for several reasons. First, you will need time away from the hustle and bustle of school life to think reflectively and freely about your essays. Secondly, some of you will find that reading all the essay prompts beforehand may hamper your creativity. Finally, the longer you've had time to percolate your ideas, the more flavorful your final brew will be. Moreover, the main Common Application essay prompts, being sufficiently broad and varied, allow you to tweak your essays to fit one of the prompts.

Myth # 4: Unless you have a pressing problem that needs explaining, you should not answer the "optional essay."

Not true. If you wish to be competitive, the so-called "optional" essay is in fact a requirement. Of course, if there is an aspect of your application that needs explaining (ex. a striking dip in your grades), the optional essay is a good place to do so. For example, one of my students used this optional essay to explain how she lost her father to cancer in her freshman year and then how her mother came down with leukemia in the following year, all of which contributed to her grades dipping in her sophomore year. If you are going to write a hardship essay, however, it is critical to write with the proper tone. Your essay should focus on how you overcame your challenges. Christina, who lost her father to cancer, described her hardship as unsentimentally as she could, and the mainstay of her reflection focused on how she grew through her challenges and what she learned about herself in the process. But for most of you, the optional essay is an opportunity to focus on yet another aspect of what makes you unique.

Myth # 5: When writing about why you want to go to college X, you can go to the website and use the promotional language provided on the school web site.

Using laudatory, promotional language to describe the school is a sure fire way of losing your reader's interest. Stay away from the verbiage of glossy marketing magazines that schools put out. When you use promotional language, you are merely filling up space with empty words and not really explaining why *you* are interested in attending college X. Instead, research the school and state why the biochemistry program, say, at this school stands out as the best fit for you. Give very specific reasons. It is not enough to say that you look forward to the opportunity to conduct undergraduate research – you have to say which lab you want to work in, and under what professor, and why. And don't leave it at that. Write about how you look forward to joining the microfinance organization on campus. You might also mention that New Haven offers you the opportunity to continue volunteering with at-risk teens. Your reply to *why this school* should demonstrate that you are committed to attending school X if you are admitted. Remember that it is in the interest of the schools to admit students who are more likely to take up their offer of admission, since their yields factor prominently into their rankings.

How to Read the Prompts

Whether long or short, the first order of business is to get over how boring the essay prompts sound. With the exception of a few such as the one from University of Chicago that asks you to w*rite about Wednesday*, students are often surprised by how utterly uninspiring they appear. The strength of your response then depends largely on how creatively you are able to render the prompt. Consider the prompt: *Write about a significant person who has had an influence on you.* Predictably, students typically choose to write about a heroic figure in the classic sense of the word. They write about someone who has shown them what it means to be a "winner." The usual suspects come to the fore: Martin Luther King, Jr., Steve Jobs, or Abraham Lincoln. Jeannette, on the other hand, wrote about her uncle who suffers from a debilitating mental illness. She begins, "*My mother used to tell me that she could stick her fingernail into the walls of my grandparent's house and the dust from the plaster would come crumbling down.*" As indicated by the tone set in this first sentence, the special person in her life is no hero in the conventional sense: *My uncle never left the house. Dropped out of college. Never married.* He was only capable of *one-sided conversations.* The influence he has had on her, then, is subtler, for she is trying to grapple with what it means to encounter someone decidedly different. She demonstrates considerable empathy and compassion as she comes to terms with her uncle, a prisoner of his mental landscape. In the process, she goes far in making herself vulnerable to a comparison between her uncle and herself, questioning the distinction between sanity and insanity.

Another way to get at the prompt is *to look beyond it.* Writing prompts are like brainteasers. Consider the following riddle: *This person has legally married two different people on the same day. Who is this person?* Most of you would associate the word "marry" with becoming wed to a partner. Your mind naturally latches onto the most familiar and prevalent use of the word "marry." When you let go of the initial interpretation, then you can *root out a slightly more obscure meaning* of the word marry, which is what priests and other religious clerics do for couples about to wed. The answer to the puzzle is *a priest.* In many ways, answering a college essay prompt is like solving a riddle: you need to look beyond your initial interpretation. For example, consider the prompt from Stanford asking, *What matters to you?* Lynette, admitted early action to Stanford, replied:

What matters is matter. Matter has mass and volume. Ninety-six percent of human matter is composed of simply carbon, oxygen, nitrogen, and hydrogen. Four mere elements create the majority of the matter of us. Whether American, Chinese,

Democratic, Republican, religious, atheist, young, old, rich, or poor we are all made of the same stuff. The differential in personality or disposition between us does not come close to the massive, enigmatic, and mystifying similarities we possess as matter. Across oceans, through time, and across physiological differences, our basic biological makeup connects us. We are all related. We then have an obligation as congruent elemental creations to help, comfort, and serve one another because of this indefinable, irrevocable, and universal interrelation. Granting each other the respect, dignity, and compassion that every single person deserves is necessary. In the name of this awesome matter that holds us together, excessive acts of generosity are called for. Merely giving one another basic human rights and respect solves the vast number of domestic, economic, and political injustices consuming us right now. We who constitute the most intelligent form of matter on earth owe it to ourselves to make generosity our top priority. Our matter is what matters in making a difference. That is what matters to me.

In the above passage, Lynette begins by thinking differently about the word "matter." Taking advantage of the second meaning of *matter* as a noun, she ponders matter in its most elemental biochemical sense. She amply demonstrates her ability to take a rather prosaic question and turn it into a clever, entertaining, and insightful passage. In so doing, she escapes the proverbial trap of delivering a dry and academic reflection about the predictably grave problems of our day.

Similarly, when answering the prompt about what you read and how it influenced you, don't limit yourself to books. Maybe you were struck by an ad you once saw at the airport, graffiti emblazoned on a wall, or a line from a poem. Avoid sounding overly serious, cultured, or studious. Typical answers to the Yale prompt about what you'd do with a free afternoon range from curling up with a favorite book, listening to music, exercising, baking a pie, or hanging out with friends. While all these are perfectly fine things to do with a free afternoon, none of them stand out as much as Colton's dream of a free afternoon: *I'd put on my purple tie, gather some daffodils, and promenade down Camino Diablo until someone falls in love with me."* In mere twenty-one words, he conveyed *character*. You can deduce that he is imaginative, self-assured, bold, humorous, and charming. In the same spirit, when asked what was the best compliment he received and from whom, he responded, *"You are an honest man, Colton—Abraham Lincoln."* The prompt never said that it had to come from someone who was alive and it never said that it had to be true. Colton's tongue-in-cheek answer is much better than the back door bragging that this prompt usually elicits.

In summary, read the prompt first and note what it is asking you to do. Then reject your first reading of the prompt. If you can imagine someone else writing something similar, then you are barking up the wrong tree. Instead, look for an unusual reading of the prompt that allows you to give a one-of-a-kind response.

CHAPTER **Nine**

Stage One--Brainstorming

"It is easier to tone down a wild idea than to think up a new one."- Alex Osborn, who coined the term *brainstorming*

COME AUGUST IN Korea, terrific monsoons would roar in flooding the streams and downing power lines. On the eve of the storm farmers would point to the moon with the soft ring around it. I too learned to watch for signs. Cats scratched behind their ears. Babies blew raspberries; birds flew closer to the ground, eschewing the discomfort that comes with the low barometric pressure at higher altitudes. My mother would complain of a dull headache. Unmindful of all the havoc sure to come in its path, I reveled in knowing something out of the ordinary was about to happen. Hopping from room to room I'd announce the coming storm as though delivering an invitation to a party. This excitement just before a storm is exactly the way I feel embarking on a new writing project.

The term brainstorm aptly describes this initial stage of writing when the sky is the limit. Cognitively speaking, that means entertaining unlikely pairing of items to create new meaning. Discovery is central to this initial stage of writing. It invites freshness and new insight. Without this stage, what results is a tired old essay. Scientists have uncovered that, indeed, just before a storm something is in the air, heightening our sense of wellbeing. Generated naturally by evaporating water, negative ions are moisture-laden particles that carry electricity. They are plentiful near any moving bodies of water like waterfalls and oceans. The healthful benefits of negative ions have been proven to be good for the brain, the heart, and the immune system, because they bind with free radicals in your body that trigger aging. Is that why so many writers say that their best ideas come in the middle of a warm shower? Brainstorming aptly describes the process of generating ideas for your essay.

Brainstorming is not primarily rational. This creative process is defined as divergent thinking. Divergent thinking, characteristic of the primary stage of writing, pairs seemingly unrelated things together. Without this unusual adjoining of ideas, your essay will lack vitality. The most common mistake students make is in not spending enough time engaging in divergent thinking. There will come a time when you will have to get hard-nosed, revising and stream-lining your thinking—a process otherwise known as convergent thinking--but during the brainstorming stage, you imbue your essay with life.

At this stage it is important not to think too much. You have to be dumb in order to see something new. Make friends with your unconscious and turn off your rationality; lend your ear to the depths of your unconscious. Dare to go to places you'd rather not during the light of day. For my student Joanne that place is the ocean. Somewhere between fascination and fear is where she begins to write. When she writes, she is relaxed and yet attentive. Perched on the lookout post, seeing through her binoculars she is all eyes and ears.

In the following passage, Joanne in a focused free write

reflects on her complex relationship to the sea, a topic that eventually gives way to her essay:

My sister is coddling a sea cucumber a hundred feet below sea level. It is not dark. *She assures me,* So much to see. *But I am more like Pip, spooked by the sheer absence, the not seeing. On a whale-watching expedition, the sea churning 3 feet-high waves, my stomach moving into my throat; like Ahab, I thought to conquer my fear of going under.* Move with the waves, *my sister hollers from the upper deck not at all green like me. I once read in my psychology textbook this quote from Jung: "Shun the unconscious and become a neurotic." My sister the amphibian bridges land and sea. In my dreams, I live on the shore waking to the roaring sea, trying to imagine a calm below the depths all manner of things undulating to a strange rhythm.*

Free writes and focused free writes are critical to the brainstorming stage. In free writing you are turning off your rational faculties as much as that is possible. Free writing is the perfect tonic for brainstorming. It is the practice of scribbling down your words as quickly as possible. It is the act of following your mind and faithfully recording what passes through it. Write as though in a trance. A student once aptly described the mindset behind free writing as freewheeling. Do mental cartwheels in the air. During a brainstorm, you have no time to mind rules about punctuation, grammar, or syntax. The key is to get the words out as quickly as possible, for as soon as you pause, you allow your self-editing voice to creep in. In the above passage about the sea, Joanne cleaned up her document a bit before sharing it with me, but the gist of her thinking all came to her in a matter of 20 minutes. Turning off her rational function allowed her to merge Captain Ahab and Jung with sea cucumbers.

From morning till night, you walk around in control of your mental faculties. In fact it is only when you get ready for bed that you turn off this powerful censor that keeps you ever on your toes. The right temporal lobe of the cortex, devoted to multisensory integration, is what keeps you in check. In *fronto-temporal* dementia, when this area in the brain deteriorates at a rapid pace, nothing is repressed. Many patients suffering from this type of dementia turn into compulsive artists. Art-making provides the channel for their new-found desire to create. You can simulate turning off the right temporal lobe by free writing. Try some free write sessions just before you fall asleep, when the prefrontal cortex shuts itself down preparing your mind for the dream state; or just after you awake when you are emerging from your dream state. Your rationality, however helpful it may be in navigating your day, will not help you to come up with new ideas. It does not help you produce novel solutions to age-old questions.

Here is how you start free writing. Begin by writing non-stop for five minutes; don't lift your fingers from the keyboard or your pen from the page. Just keep writing. Don't stop to ponder what you've written, to make corrections, to look up a word's meaning, or to check spelling. Forget the rules of formal English. It may help you to have a timer on hand. While you are writing, just pay attention to the movie in your mind. Don't lead but be led. You don't have to worry about saying anything significant. Simply write what comes to mind no matter how seemingly trivial or inconsequential. Don't worry if your writing lacks clear connection, meaning, organization, or punctuation. If you find yourself stuck for lack of something to say, just keep repeating the last word you have written or write, "I'm stuck" until a fresh thought emerges. After a few minutes, the results may not be pretty but you will have started writing.

What should you do with your free write? Over time, they will deliver over a word, a line, or a thought that is worth noting. That may become the basis of your essay topic. But even if it does not deliver a topic for your essay, it will help to put you in a limber frame of mind for writing.

Don't worry if free writes don't come easily to you the first time. It will take some practice before you get comfortable with it. So be patient. Try doing a free write twice a day and then increase to 3 or 4 a day. Remember that you only need 5 minutes (which you can increase to 10 or longer later) for each session. Once you've identified a topic for your essay, it may help you then to move into a "focused" free write, free-associating with a particular word or a notion.

CHAPTER Ten

Stage Two—First Draft

"It was ten pages long. It wasn't called anything, just a rhythm thing on paper," Bob Dylan on writing the draft of *Like a Rolling Stone*.

AFTER BRAINSTORMING, YOU come away with an inkling. By that, I mean an idea that persists. Or you may land upon a possible essay when rummaging through your notebook, thumbing through your free writes, or reading the cereal box during breakfast. By whichever means the topic comes to you, you know you have a potential topic at hand because it excites you. That is to say, it elicits an emotional reaction. Now you are ready to commit your idea to your first draft.

The first draft is not your life partner. Beginning writers sometimes assume that there can be only one first draft. In fact, there can be multiple first drafts. Like free writing, you have to get it out fast—albeit this time sticking to your topic at hand. The half-life of an inkling is not very long. Don't try to craft lovely sentences. Don't even worry about transitions. The goal is to get it down on a page so that you can have a look at it. Trying to revise or edit your piece in this stage may result in a serious writing block. Writing quickly will enable you to be more honest as you commit yourself to first thoughts. You can only say something new if you allow yourself to be raw.

When composing the first draft, I usually use legal-sized paper and write by hand. I like having margins on both sides so that I can loop in new inserts or make marginal comments. I don't worry about the clever beginning lines or an artful conclusion yet. I am simply intent upon getting the shape of the thing down on paper so that I can play with it.

CHAPTER Eleven

Stage Three—Revision

"Throw up into your typewriter every morning. Clean up every noon." –Raymond Chandler

IF YOUR FIRST draft feels sprightly, then you are ready to craft your essay. If, however, your draft has somehow lost that quality or fails to engage you sufficiently, you need to either write more drafts or go back to brainstorming. Assuming you are ready for the next stage, you will now begin to take the essay in sections and revise it the way an interior decorator goes about redesigning. Revising, as the name implies, involves taking a serious second look at your draft. It is like remodeling rather than merely tidying up your living room. So it might involve rearranging all the furniture, rolling up the carpet, and retiring that uninspiring lamp shade for good. Revising invites you to re-imagine the piece.

But it requires a different kind of creativity from the wide-open stance that you assumed when you conceived the piece. Now you are going to zoom in and close the circle. You are not looking for new materials as much as pruning and fine-tuning what you already have. Precision and craft become central. In short, you are checking for consistency, flow, and logic.

It is critical to get some distance from your draft. You should read it out loud and/or have someone else read it out loud for you. Then ask yourself if what you hear is the right word, or if it carries the intended tone. Mark every word or a phrase that makes you think twice or gives you pause. Does that second sentence follow naturally from the first? And does it lead seamlessly into your third? Did you provide sufficient transitions between paragraphs? Don't lose steam now! Revise with gusto!

After you have a workable structure, organization, and narrative continuity you are now ready to put in the nuts and bolts. To that end we turn to elements of good writing.

Twelve

Elements of Good Writing

WRITING STYLE IS the manner that the author uses to connect with her audience. Style says much about the author's voice and personality as well as her perception of the audience. Style encompasses diction, syntactical structure, and rhythm as well as the *feel* conveyed in the prose. A skilled writer taking advantage of stylistic opportunities can turn just about any topic into an engaging read, while an unskilled writer can take a potentially engaging story and turn it into a sleeper. To illustrate, I took a passage from Hemingway's *Farewell to Arms* and doctored it by changing the wording here and there while staying true to the intended meaning. Notice the difference between the two versions. Here is the original version.

> *Troops went by the house and down the road and the dust they raised powdered the leaves of the trees. The trunks of the trees too were dusty and the leaves fell early that year and we saw the troops marching along the road and the dust rising and leaves, stirred by the breeze, falling and the soldiers marching and afterward the road bare and white except for the leaves.*

In the above passage, you experience directly and power-fully the scene cinematically rendered by Hemingway. It flows like the endless marching he describes. There is not a word that you could take away without changing the mood or meaning. Concision, rhythm, and variation of sentence structure combine to lend vitality to the writing. In contrast, see what happens in the doctored version below:

There were many troops who went by the house and down the road. With their heavy boots they caused a lot of commotion and raising dust, covered the leaves with a fine layer of powder. The dust was so heavy at times that it even covered up the trunks of the trees. In part because of the heavy settling of dust on the leaves and in part because of the stirring from the breeze—instigated by all the marching, the leaves fell early that year. Mainly, what we remember is the constant marching and how afterward the road was bare and white except for the leaves on the ground.

The version I doctored does not attend to rhythm: it is clunky and wordy. With poor choice in diction such as *"instigate,"* I create distance between the reader and the scene described. Good form or style like your favorite song must be not only in-viting but also musical. When you analyze a good piece of mu-sic, you find balance, rhythm, harmony, and flow--all of which translate into a pleasant sound. Similarly identifiable elements go into writing an essay with great style.

Listen to your writing

Continuing with the metaphor of song, consider the parallels between music and writing. We use punctuation to direct and punctuate the flow of the essay. Periods demarcate one complete unit of thought from the next. Colons anticipate what is to come by way of explanation, a list or examples. Semicolons suggest a connection or a consequence. Commas separate items in a series. Dashes add flare—albeit tangential to the core subject. And the exclamation point speaks with gusto. In reading out loud, you hear the way writing is supposed to sound. What sounds pleasing, it so happens, is also clear, concise, and coherent. Punctuation and grammar rules exist to connect sound and sense.

Vary your sentence structure and length

Reading out loud will also help you to ferret out dead places created by unvaried sentence construction. Without variation, your essay, however exciting the topic, will sink. It would be like hearing the repetition of the same melody with no end.

You should know your sentence types so that you can comfortably use a variety of sentence structures. A **phrase** is a grouping of words without a subject or an independent verb such as *inside the house, to run away, or listening to the sound*—respectively called *prepositional, infinitive,* and *participial phrase.*

A **clause,** however, has a subject and a verb as in *the boy hit the ball* or *after she ran for president.* If in the second example, you changed it to *after running for president,* then it is no longer a clause but a participial phrase because it is missing a subject and does not contain an independent verb. Clauses are of two types: *independent* and *dependent clause,* which are sometimes known as *main clause* and *subordinate clause.* A main clause is in fact a complete sentence because it has a subject and a verb expressing a unit of thought. The above example—*the boy hit the ball*—can stand alone if you choose to put a period after the last word *ball.* On the other hand, the clause *after she ran for president* cannot stand alone because it begins with the subordinating conjunction *after*, which makes it dependent. Other examples of subordinating conjunctions include *although, since, while,* and *for.*

The four basic kinds of **grammatical sentences** are the following: *simple, compound, complex,* and *compound-complex.* A simple sentence consists of a single main clause as in *I studied for my chemistry test.* A compound sentence has two main clauses joined by a coordinating conjunction such as *and, but,* and *or. For* example, *I can go to you, or you can come over.* A comma before the coordinating conjunction usually sets off the two clauses. A complex sentence contains a subordinate clause and a main clause: *After I write my book, I will take a long vacation.* Finally, a compound-complex sentence as you might imagine contains two main clauses and a subordinating clause: *Although I ran to the bus stop, I missed the bus, and I had to call a cab.*

The examples below demonstrate the effect sentence variation has on the narrative style. This passage comes from *Charlotte's Web:*

> *Fern came slowly down the stairs. Her eyes were red from crying. As she approached her chair, the carton wobbled, and there was a scratching noise. Fern looked at her father. Then, she lifted the lid of the carton. There, inside, looking up at her was the new-born pig. It was a white one. The morning light shone through its ears turning them pink.*

Now see what happens in the version I've doctored below:

> *Fern came slowly down the stairs. Her eyes were red from crying. She approached her chair, and the carton wobbled. There was a scratching noise. Fern looked at her father. Then she lifted the lid of the carton. The*

*new-born pig looked up at her from inside the carton.
It was a white one. The morning light shown through its
ears and it turned them pink.*

In the doctored example, a string of simple, declarative sentences without variation sounds dull and monotonous. It has no rhythm. The momentous occasion of a birthing turns into a humdrum event. In the original text, you have the following pattern: Simple, Simple, Compound-complex, Simple, Simple (beginning with adverb of time), Simple (beginning with adverb of place, followed by a participial phrase), Simple, Simple (ending with a prepositional phrase).

While repetitive sentence structures can be useful for rhetorical effect as in Martin Luther King Jr.'s "I have a dream" speech, unintended repetitions make for boring writing. In a paragraph, you can have simple sentences, followed by sentences beginning with a subordinate clause, or one ending with a subordinate clause. You can have compound sentences followed by a complex sentence that qualifies or explains, then with the addition of a short, short sentence, you might affect a dramatic closure. Variation of sentence constructions keeps your reader interested.

Imitate the spoken word

In the personal essay mimicking spoken language helps to create an intimate tone. Consider the difference in the *feel* between the two: A) *I went into 6th grade with a sense of terror that only manifests out of the looming possibility of perpetual loneliness.* Or B) *I will never forget the terrifying loneliness I felt at the beginning of sixth grade as the new kid in town.* Imitating the spoken word means using words that are familiar and direct as opposed to stiff, long, or abstract. Good writing is clear, direct, and personal: truthful, not sentimental. A familiar style, however, is not the same as a breezy, self-conscious tone: *Now let me tell you, as the family historian, about my famous uncle—the Albanian lieutenant—the bravest man in all of Eastern Europe.* Pretentious and somewhat condescending, this manner of speaking puts everyone to sleep. Imitating the spoken word also does not mean that you can do away with conventions of proper writing. For example, you can't use unusual contractions such as *that's* or *you'll*, or adopt colloquialisms such as *they're not cool with that,* unless you are quoting. The following passage is taken from a student's early draft of his college application essay. Notice the difference between examples A & B. Which paragraph is more inviting to you? Which paragraph warms you to the author? Which is more direct?

EXAMPLE A:

The three happy rings of the lunch bell marked the beginning of a thirty-five minute respite from school, during which students were free to run carefree around the schoolyard. Finally, the moment I had looked forward to all day had arrived. Breaking away from the throng of hungry stampeding children, I ran into the band room. Nearly deserted, I let my fingers burst forth in rapturous melody.

EXAMPLE B:

I couldn't wait for the lunch bell. While the bell for my friends signaled running around for half an hour, I had my heart set on working my fingers. Fighting the hungry crowd, I ran to the band room. There I sat and played the piano to my heart's content.

The first version is lengthier than the second—67 words versus 50. In reading it out loud, you can hear how stilted and distant the language sounds in the first example. No one you know says things like *"three happy rings marks the beginning…"* or *"I let my fingers burst forth in rapturous melody."* Moreover, note the misplaced modifier in the last sentence: *nearly deserted, I….* Surely, he means to say that the music room and not he was nearly deserted. Just by mimicking speech, we come closer to a natural sound and in the process knock off 17 words. Wordiness translates to stilted writing. Good writing is always concise, direct, clear, and accessible.

Use parallel construction to express congruent thoughts

Parallel constructions allow the reader to see more easily the similar content. See, for example, the parallel construction in the famous biblical passage from Ecclesiastics 3:1-2.

> *There is a time for everything,*
> *and there is a season for every activity under heaven.*
> *A time to be born*
> *And a time to die*
> *A time to plant*
> *And a time to uproot*

In the following example, see what happens when you have a loose construction expressing coordinate elements using variegated form: *During fasting, the body metabolizes its own protein, releases ketones into the blood stream, and the body is more prone to dehydration. The ideas presented lose a bit of their cogency and concision.* Using parallel construction, to the contrary, lends greater cohesion and clarity: *During fasting, the body metabolizes its own protein, releases ketones into the blood stream, and becomes dehydrated.*

Choose short words

It may sound counterintuitive, but short words are more powerful than long words when telling a story. Many students try to impress by using big vocabulary words. However, *begin* is more powerful than *commence*. *Brave* is stronger than *courageous*. In achieving a more personable and powerful style, opting for short words will deliver more fuel than choosing long ones. Elaborate words often sound pretentious and self-conscious. Generally speaking, Anglo-Saxon words tend to be more inviting and direct than Latin words. Let your ear be your guide. See the passage from the *National Geographic* below:

> *Animal protein, insofar as bonobos get any, had seemed to come mainly from insects and millipedes. But Fruth and Hohmann reported nine cases of hunting by bonobos at Lomako, seven of which involved sizable duikers, usually grabbed by one bonobo, ripped apart at the belly while still alive, with the entrails eaten first, and the meat shared.*

Compare the original now with my doctored version:

> *Animal protein, insofar as bonobos acquire any, had appeared to derive largely from insects and millipedes. But Fruth and Hohmann counted nine cases of hunting by bonobos at Lomako, seven of which involved gargantuan duikers, usually obtained by one bonobo, torn away roughly from the belly while still alive, with the entrails masticated first, and the meat divided and consumed.*

Ripped has more immediacy than *torn away roughly*; *get* is more powerful than *acquired*; *grabbed* is better than *obtained*; and *eaten* is more raw than *masticated*.

Keep modifiers close to what they are modifying

Avoid confusion and ambiguity by placing modifiers close to what they are modifying. Just by moving the words around, you can achieve clarity. You don't mean to say: *Hanging from a tree, my mother saw the bat.* You do mean to say: *My mother saw the bat hanging from the tree.*

Prefer the active voice and know when to use the passive

Use *active voice* to emphasize the subject performing the action. *The boy hit the ball* is more directed, concise, and empathic than the *passive voice*: *The ball was hit by the boy.* Generally speaking, you will want to use the active voice to energize your narrative, although there are some instances when you will want to emphasize the receiver of the action. You can easily change a passive construction to an active one simply by identifying the receiver of the action and figuring out the doer of the action. For example: *An attempt was made to reach out to the refugees to figure out why there was no progress on their health,* can be turned around to the following: *We attempted to reach out to the refugees to understand better the causes behind their ill health.*

Reserve the punch line for the end of the sentence

The sentence is like a mini-story; as such, it is better to end it with a bang than a whimper. With jokes, it is customary to save the punch line for the end: in writing, reserve the most emphatic words for last. Punctuating your sentence with a period signals the dramatic closure to a story or a unit of thought. For the example below, if you want to place emphasis on the weight of the gorillas you will want to say, *The Bengali gorillas can grow to be over 200 pounds.* But if you want to stress the fact that they are from Bengal, you will write instead, *The 200 pound gorillas live in Bengal.*

Use strong verbs

Without strong verbs, your sentences will be dull or dead. They will fail to relay the meaning you intend. All the adverbs or phrases in the world will not save an imprecise, inactive, or inappropriately chosen verb. The rest of your sentence is merely assisting like a rower to the sea captain at the helm. If chosen wisely, your verb will reduce the number of words you need to get your meaning across and it will energize your writing like nothing else can. It will sharpen the meaning, create movement, and engage your reader. So don't just *walk* when you can *waddle, saunter, meander, sidle, shuffle,* or *dash.* And don't just *look* when you can *gawk, peer, spy,* or *probe.* Here's a hint: you know you can do better when you see those –ly words. Did your brother *eat ravenously* or did he *wolf* down his food? Did the old man *walk cautiously* or did he *pace* himself? Adverbs are often the weakest link in a sentence. Get rid of them.

Keep subjects and verbs close together

Too much distance between the subject and verb causes confusion. No more than one modifier closely tied to the subject should come between the subject and verb. Consider: *Kicking and screaming the boy caught stealing candy from the dime store was shamed in front of the crowd,* as compared to *The boy kicking and screaming, caught stealing from the candy store was shamed in front of the crowd.* In the second example, the distance between the subject and verb makes it hard for the reader to remember who or what was the subject. All the material between the subject and verb delays the action and makes for dense reading.

Be careful about modifiers

Unless they shed new light on the subject, adverbs and adjectives can weigh a sentence down. For example, notice the following sentence. *The sun shone brightly red against the dark sky.* The modifiers in the example above do not significantly change the scene described in the sentence. That is, the sun shines *red* particularly at dusk and the sky is often *dark* at this time, and *brightly* hardly says anything new about the way the sun shines. If you are going to use an adjective, for example, make it worthwhile, as in, *Sidling along the wharf, the cunning otter regularly helped himself to the fishmonger's bin of choice trout.*

Avoid wordiness

All the stylistic points thus far mentioned ask you to be economic with words. Wordiness creates dead places in writing. The litmus test for wordiness is asking yourself: will knocking off this word change the intended meaning of the sentence? You can subtract words by changing *clauses* into *phrases or into simple past participles.*

You can find a list of commonly used expressions that make your writing wordy in *Elements of Style* by Strunk & White. Go over the list before you embark on your revision. The following is a sampling taken from Strunk and White's book of style:

Wordy	Better
the question as to whether	*whether*
there is no doubt but that	*no doubt*
used for fuel purposes	*used for fuel*
in a hasty manner	*hastily*

this is a subject that	*this subject*
Her story is a strange one.	*Her story is strange.*
the reason why is that	*because*
owing to the fact that	*since (because)*
call your attention to the fact that	*notify you*
I was unaware of the fact that	*I was unaware*
the fact that he had not succeeded	*his failure*
He was not very often on time.	*He usually came late.*

Avoid choppy sentences: use appositives

An appositive is a word or a phrase usually set off by commas describing or modifying the noun or subject that precedes it. Appositives allow for combining choppy sentences into one by splicing the one sentence into the other. Example A: *The team proposed to amend the one roll-one-turn rule. The team was unfairly judged for making multiple rolls per turn.* These two choppy sentences can be combined in the example B: *The team, unfairly judged for making multiple rolls per turn, proposed to amend the one-roll-per-turn rule.*

Show don't Tell

Just about every book on writing will tell you to show but don't tell. Students often ask me what that means. It means conveying your feelings without telling about them. Use analogies such as metaphors or similes and keen description to convey your sentiment. Find words involving all the senses. Don't tell your reader about the story, but directly relay the story putting yourself squarely in it. Don't say that you are hard-working, disciplined, enthusiastic, creative, or innovative; rather, show it by telling the story of how you snuck into the lab after hours to check on the Drosophila flies. See how in example A, telling about the experience is not as convincing as showing it in example B. Example A: *During my time at the lab, I learned about patience and perseverance.* Example: B: *Suspecting something amiss in the procedure, I set out like Sherlock Holmes to repeat the experiment not once but twice and found to my delight that the faulty gene did express itself in the third generation.*

Detailing

Think about the things you care about. You didn't choose your partner because he is generically a good person. And you didn't bring home your cat because he is like any other. You chose your boyfriend because the first time you laid eyes on him, he was walking down the street with his headphones, oblivious, and you just knew. To this day, two school dances later, you still love the way he builds castles in the air. And it was love at first sight when you met Moo-Moo with his front paws split black and white down the middle and the telltale bad-boy tear on his right ear. Detailing makes things come alive. Notice how this sentence just doesn't catch your attention: *She walked into the room with a shocking dress and people took note.* It lacks the pointed clarity and drama of the following remake: *Wearing a red halter dress with green polka dots, she made her grand entrance like a diva as heads turned in disbelief.* If you don't fill in the details, your reader will lose interest. A student wrote about an auspicious kick that scored him an unexpected win: *The impact sent a satisfying jolt through my fibular and femur and a resounding "POOM" through the air."* How unremarkable if he had simply written:

"It was a very powerful kick."

Detailing done well is like the perfect accouterment to your outfit. There is nothing more distasteful than a gaudy necklace or a loud scarf to cheapen your classy black dress. Similarly in writing, detailing is effective if it provides just the right accent. An example of an overdone detail might look something like this: *Lost in ecstasy, my fingers broke out in song.* Such a sentence reeks of melodrama. When overdone, the reader loses patience, interest, and focus: in short, you lose your audience. Likewise, a detail can't be drab; it should surprise and delight your reader. And it should not go on with no end in sight. Remember, you don't want to be like Owl in Winnie-the-Pooh, whose prodigious storytelling, far from delighting, is a chore for anyone unlucky enough to wander into his tree house. His long-winded descriptions make for dense reading. So involved are his details that even he on occasion gets lost in his telling, asking famously, "Now, where was I?" Practice detailing judiciously, mindful of your reader's time and his tendency to snore if you go on and on about it. A good detail gives clarity and grace to your writing. It allows your reader to zoom in on an aspect that gives meaning to the greater whole. When Franz Kafka, for example, tells his reader that Gregor Samsa in the novel *Metamorphosis* has turned into a cockroach, we can hardly believe otherwise: *His numerous legs, which were pitifully thin compared to the rest of his bulk, flickered helplessly before his eyes,"* [as he lay] *"on his hard, as it were armor-plated back and when he lifted a little he could see his domelike brown belly divided into stiff arched segments."* You will not doubt him when Kafka tells you, *"It was no dream."* Detailing mimics your visual memory and gives immediate access to the event at hand. Choosing the right details will add color, draw attention to what is essential, and help set the tone for your story.

Writing by Analogy

All that was said about elements of good writing can be summed up in a word—poetry. Poetry is about creating new meaning through analogy. When it does not suffice to say that the full moon was large, then you can say that the full moon was as large as an extra-large pizza. But don't stop there, talk about how on account of the moon you took a detour and drove up the hill by the golf course for a second look and came home to burnt chicken. In short, all good writing tends toward poetry. Consider *Ars Poetica*, an instructive poem by Archibald MacLeish.

A poem should be palpable and mute
As a globed fruit, dumb
As old medallions to the thumb
Silent as the sleeve-worn stone
Of casement ledges where the moss has grown
A poem should be wordless
As the flight of birds
A poem should be motionless in time
As the moon climbs
Leaving, as the moon releases
Twig by twig the night-entangled trees
Leaving, as the moon behind the winter leaves
Memory by memory the mind
A poem should be motionless in time
As the moon climbs
A poem should be equal to not true
For all the history of grief
An empty doorway and a maple leaf
For love, the leaning grasses and two lights above the sea
A poem should not mean but be.

If you substitute "poem" for good writing, you have in this poem all the ingredients of good writing. It says that good writing uses sensory language without drawing attention to the words themselves. Using analogy, writers show how words signify but how words themselves are as silent as *a flight of birds.* Notice how his metaphors such as *medallions to the thumb or casement ledges where moss has grown* infuse emotion into rational understanding. MacLeish goes on to explain through analogy how good writing or poetry is what approximates but is not equal to what we experience as reality; for in truth, good writing seeks to make sense of, say, our grief, which could best be described by *an empty doorway and a maple leaf* and love as *leaning grasses.* Moreover, he reminds the reader that good writing awakens the senses. Finally, good writing does not explain but simply lets be.

CHAPTER Thirteen

Twenty Most Common Pitfalls in Writing the College Admissions Essay

1. *Dishonesty:* You are dishonest when you try to be some-one else or write what you think you ought to say. Your writing either rings true or false. Truth is often surprising and strange.

2. *Obtuse Thinking:* Fuzzy thinking engenders poor writing. Clarity of thought is a product of patience. Don't rush headlong into your piece without thinking it through. Good writing is precise.

3. *Selling Yourself:* Lured by what you perceive to be a win-ning topic, some of you will be tempted to write about something that does not move or interest you. Don't sell yourself short. Write about what invigorates!

4. *Prone to Exaggeration:* Exaggerated claims annoy your readers, and cause them to lose their interest or their trust in you. When it comes to writing about emotionally charged moments, it is better to curb your emotions.

5. *Ambiguity:* Your desire for closure may at times force you to draw conclusions that may not ring true. Unlike the SAT essay, the personal essay is all about the gray

area. Admit to ambiguity or leave things open-ended if that is where you honestly stand.

6. *Answer the Question:* Don't assume that Yale will not notice that you are really answering the Stanford prompt. Answer the question put before you.

7. *The Never-Ending Introduction:* Don't take up too many lines creating the opening scene. Like an orchestra forever tuning its instruments, the beginning paragraph sometimes takes far too long to get to the story. In a great majority of first drafts, the introductory paragraph undergoes a drastic cut.

8. *A Sliver not the Whole Pie:* Let go of your need to put too much into one essay. An essay with too many prongs will appear disorganized and disjunctive. Stick to one main point and go deep exploring that one main idea.

9. *Sticking with Generalities:* The lackluster essay referencing the "black cat" or the "weird day" says nothing to distinguish what makes your cat unique or what happened to make your day seem strange. Make your writing come to life with vivid attention to details.

10. *Don't Offend Your Reader:* Because you don't know your reader intimately, it is best to avoid certain topics, lest you offend. Though I am generally not fond of lists, the following topics should be avoided in 99 percent of cases: divorce, romantic relationships, political allegiance, religious faith, and bodily functions.

11. *Stereotypical Story:* Avoid the typical story with a predictable plot. Here is the litmus test of uniqueness: if you can imagine someone else writing something like it, then it says nothing new about you. It will be hard for you to stand out.

12. *Flow:* A good essay is like a song. Such an essay gives the

semblance of ease and continuity between sentences and paragraphs.

13. *Stilted:* By your tone, you can invite or offend your reader. Avoid the use of language that is either too self-conscious or pretentious. Choose simplicity and clarity over obfuscation. Note how in the following sentence the stilted tone also renders the meaning of the sentence unclear: *I've had the real privilege of absorbing the wealth of one intellectual treasure, whose nature compelled him to put me in proximity with many others.* Stated clearly and naturally, the writer means to say: My good friend introduced me to many people.

14. *Sloppy:* Avoid making mistakes in spelling, punctuation, or choice of words. You can often catch your mistakes when you read your essay out loud. Have someone else read it.

15. *Cohesion:* By making sure that all the points in your essay connect back to the central theme, you create cohesion. Avoid skipping steps in logic by presenting your narrative step by step.

16. *Too Many Cooks in the Kitchen:* Take ownership of your essay and avoid trying to incorporate feedback from multiple readers in your drafting stage. You can be pulled in too many directions, and you risk losing your own voice. Remember that this is an essay about you, so no one can tell it for you.

17. *Story without a Message:* Don't get carried away telling your story that you forget to state the lesson learned, unless you make it obvious in the telling of your story.

18. *Unbalanced:* Use the essays collectively as an opportunity to show your various interests, talents, and characteristics. Avoid making a reference to a topic already

discussed in another essay.

19. *Criticizing Others:* The best way to avoid criticizing others is by not comparing yourself either implicitly or explicitly with others. You don't want to appear self-righteous, narrow-minded, judging, or self-congratulating.

20. *Sentimentality:* Avoid saccharine scene descriptions, pseudo-poetic, floral language, or overly obvious analogies. Sentimental writing is poor writing because ultimately it leaves little room for your reader to figure things out on her own. Such overwrought writing tends to hammer the point home when all you have to do is simply nudge it in.

CHAPTER Fourteen

Winning Essays

I OPEN WITH this piece you've encountered already, when I discussed the shape of the essay, because it models the classic story line. It starts with a vivid scene that sets the tone and provides the metaphor of the journey. It also manages to take what could be a trite topic—a Boy Scout venture—into something unexpected and thoughtful. The author weaves effortlessly in and out of story and reflection.

Beaver Damnation

As the sun burns through the fog, my fellow comrades and I trudge through chest deep mud, beleaguered and fatigued. The weight of the eighty-pound canoe upon my shoulders sends waves of muscle pinching pain. Upon the eleventh hour, patience becomes myth, and every sinew in my body focuses on the finish line. This is Northern Tier country, forty minutes outside of Bissett, Canada, a place scouts have come to call Heartbreak.

Northern Tier offers breath-taking views of crystal lakes and eternally green treetops. With beauty comes a price, however, and before a scout may reach salvation, he must encounter his final test, one of the toughest terrains known to mankind.

I've come from a world that has little remorse for those who are not prepared, and scouting has shaped my life to always expect the unexpected. Northern Tier provided me a bubble, isolated from the world. Every motion, every movement, every decision had a consequence, and whether the effect was positive or negative, it was exigent and real. When everything you do directly influences your next move, a new sense of clarity arises, and every detail receives an unparalleled focus. On our eighth day, with every muscle trembling with exhaustion, I reached the last portage before Beaver Damnation. As the lake came into view, I replayed the fantasy over and over again in my mind of that cathartic dropping of the canoe. Now, left or right? If I drop to my right a rock could pierce the hull of our canoe and doom us all. If I go left, a massive leech will gain an opportunity to squelch up my pant leg and latch on to my calf. The canoe's weight was unbearable. I had to choose quickly. A fellow scout yells something in my ear. Suddenly I realize I'm falling. Time's up. Feeling my body engulfed by the brisk water, I knew I had made the right choice. As we paddled across Sasiginnigak Lake, I relished the thought of having saved the day. That is, until I felt a burning pain on my shin. I hate leeches.

Every day we are plagued with insignificance. We go on autopilot and make decisions with little consequence or care. Our routines numb us to boredom. We fail to be captured by what is in front of us. My experience at Northern Tier made me realize in retrospect that I can't afford to cruise through life. Like paint to canvas, Northern Tier awakened me to a more vibrant life. Years of scouting have taught me about perseverance and presence of mind. With these lessons, I hope to further shape my life to become a man with the heart of a scout.

This is a contemplative essay about the process of art-making. The contemplative essay is a natural fit for the personal essay. This piece luxuriates in the seemingly voluminous space of the essay as the author ruminates on how and why she makes art. Note the unusual metaphors like the corn on the cobb as a mesh for the mind or the blind mole nosing his way through dirt, which turns out to be especially fitting in light of what the author says about the "grounding" aspect of art-making. Moreover, the allusion to the novel, The Brother's Karamazov, gives by analogy another dimension to understanding what the author means by art. By carefully deploying metaphors and analogies, the author writes poignantly and clearly about a topic that could be potentially overly abstract.

Nosing Our Way Through Dirt

It is hard to stay grounded in art-making. Inspiration is dizzying because the ideas it springs threatens to run amuck. The trouble is isolating the singular from the whole. Out of chaos, a thread enters my mind. Then it spins. A pattern emerges. Connecting the parts, I am in search of meaning—some insight about our mole-like, prodding existence and what it's all about. It's about unifying the sensible and the senseless, finding the link between opposing paragons, nosing our way through dirt to create tunnels between unmet halves. In the end, it's not about the search, but how I reconfigure the world and myself in it. Art is about contriving a home.

I spent last summer at Rhode Island School of Design pulling color out of plain portraits and painting them in hues of brown, red, and blue. The self-portrait eventually gave way to a relief of the artist made of hemp; she is incarcerated inside a hexagonal web of thread. Corn on the cob overlay the webbing with faces for kernels. I was trying to convey the difficulty of penetrating the filter guarding the mind. I was interested in exploring human nature at its breaking point. The idea of outside forces negatively influencing a person's filter, distorting an individual mindset, makes us seem breakable, the opposite of our conception; that we are purposeful and unflinching. In the process, I learned that this desire for certainty and security could make us prisoners of our own thoughts. I was reminded of Kolya, the young boy in *The Brothers Karamazov*, who likes to hide behind his knowledge of philosophers. Were he an artist, he might have tried to insert himself into the lot with the rest of humanity and through his own suffering uncover what it means to be human. Perhaps he lacks the courage to create himself anew; instead, he hides behind the wisdom of philosophers. I learned through art-making that truth emerges from a refusal to accept what has been merely handed down to me as truth.

It turns out that art-making is grounding after all. It is surprisingly sane. It is about finding meaning in a sea of dizzying possibilities. It is about holding out hope. It is about taking to heart Dostoyevsky's key message in *The Brothers Karamazov,* that we are somehow responsible for each other. It is about finding myself not as a singular individual but as part of a greater whole. It is about stepping out sometimes, strengthening our web of thread so we can tear through society's barrier, exposing ourselves to a world decidedly strange. Naturally, a future filled with uncertainty brings nausea because it devalues routine. But without plans, thinking becomes creating. While it would be easy for me to hide, I step out despite my fears knowing and remembering the exhilaration of finding out something I had not known about myself and feeling suddenly the world drawing a little closer to me.

MASTERING THE COLLEGE APPLICATION ESSAY

This essay retires the geriatric adjective and replaces it with phrases like "fiery piano break," "knotty harmonic structure," and "ferocious improvisation." Likewise, the description of improvisation as a cat falling out of a tree and managing to land on its feet is precious. These analogies help to drive home the point that jazz and computer programming have much in common.

Playing Celia

Bud Powell's improvised solo on "Celia" begins with a fiery piano break that still astonishes me to this day. Powell negotiates a melodic path through the knotty harmonic structure of the tune. Like a cat falling out of a tree, Bud's ferocious improvisation takes a consistently unpredictable route, yet always manages to land on its feet. After weeks of determination, I was able to match Bud's phrasing so closely that I could only hear one piano when I played along with the recording. There are two elements that are absolutely necessary to create great music. First, the composer must have a clear thought process, which comes from technical mastery and experience. Second, the composer must possess a supreme wildness of imagination. Often in art, people compromise one of these elements at the expense of the other. For example, technical perfection can render a piece of music boring and emotionless or the reverse, musical without mastery. My lessons in music inform how I approach computer engineering.

Music and computer science require a spirit of practical innovation. When I work in either medium, I encounter various problems and puzzles that demand ingenuity. As a jazz pianist, my role in a band is to support the music by providing improvised musical interjections called "fills." I believe that the best fills are both simple and effective. Often the most musical thing to do is to simply play one note with supreme confidence. When I am able to condense all the emotion, excitement, and intellect into just a few crucial notes, it gives me a musical thrill beyond anything imaginable. Computer programming is the same way.

The things that I value in good music, such as simplicity, clarity, concision, and completeness, are exactly what make for good computer code. As a programmer, I will use my logic and creativity to tackle complicated problems. When I encounter a bug in a program, I strive to write a simple yet effective algorithm to fully address the problem as gracefully as possible. Organizing a set of numbers from least to greatest is one example a computational task that I have encountered. An engineer who is methodical and logical can conceive of many different algorithms that will get the job done. However, an aesthetic sensibility is equally important in order to find the most elegant algorithm for the job at hand. Just as a strong musical statement requires both musical imagination and flawless execution, an elegant algorithm requires both ingenuity and logic.

In the following essay, the author avoids the common pitfall of boasting by staying away from any self-congratulating interjections about how hard he worked to make the project happen. He personalizes the essay with softer touches such as opening and closing the essay with Joseph's voice and interjecting the narrative with his reflections on the contending developmental theories on the African economy. The depth of his engagement with as well as the facility with which he speaks about developmental economics provides the motive for his leadership in microfinance.

Out of Africa

Watching me juggle the cob of roasted corn between my hands, Joseph takes it back from me, laughing, "Your hands are soft. You need more work in the field to get hands like mine." With that he snaps the cob in two, tosses half to me, and gestures to a seat near the fire. It's midnight, and Joseph has just finished his day's work at our guesthouse outside Nairobi. He earns two dollars a day but counts himself lucky, as most of his friends are unemployed. In response to my concern, Joseph only chuckles. "This is Africa."

My encounters in Africa were in no way unique. Anyone who spends time in the continent will come face to face with devastating, widespread poverty. We have seen billions of dollars in aid pouring in with little effect. Huge infusions of money and goods have not been able to lift the economy, and the dark side of aid – corruption and a sense of entitlement – is on the rise. Recently, the introduction of microfinance to Africa, whereby small loans are made to those without access to financial resources, may offer a solution.

In 2007, I made my first microloan to a milk farmer in Tajikistan, helping foot the bill for a dairy farmer's cow. Over the course of nine months, he paid back my loan of one hundred dollars using profits from his expanded dairy business. I reinvested his repayment to four other businesses across Africa. The simple, sustainable idea behind microfinance resonated with me in a way that charity never did – I could empower the poor through a partnership, not through handouts.

Last year, I turned my personal involvement with microfinance into a school-wide movement. I founded the Lamorinda Kiva Club with the intent of raising awareness and creating a microfinance fund that will stay with the school for years. The school district, however, had other ideas: my club was banned due to the risk involved in financial investment, despite the 99% repayment rate of loans through Kiva, an online microfinance platform. After three meetings and proposals, we were able to work out a compromise. My club would receive no support or sponsorship from the school (in the school's eyes we don't exist), but I could hold meetings and run operations from an empty classroom.

As I couldn't publicize the club in the school bulletin, I made a Facebook page, posted announcements online and held the first meeting. I gave a crash-course on microfinance to a few dozen students, explaining that money invested in the club would stay in circulation forever, flowing back and forth between the club and entrepreneurs in the developing world. By the end of my presentation, the club had pledged over $1000.00--money that will support entrepreneurs over and over again for years to come.

The club has only gained momentum throughout the school and community. It has grown from forty to one hundred and fifty members who actively manage over $5000 in loans in 40 countries. I've made presentations to schools and youth groups, designed and printed club shirts, organized successful fundraisers and secured donations from businesses. Despite the frustrating road blocks and long hours, it is exhilarating and immensely rewarding to start a community program with a global, lasting impact.

I don't delude myself. Microfinance is no silver bullet for poverty. Africa's problems are extensive and deeply rooted. In the coming years, the continent will need to formulate a comprehensive strategy that addresses government corruption, increases foreign investment, and encourages local entrepreneurship. Although daunting, this slate of tasks can be achieved with smart, efficient solutions.

It is possible that our efforts will be fruitless and poverty will drag on through the 21st century, but viewing the future through that lens is an admission of defeat. I look forward to expanding my knowledge by studying developmental economics and comparative politics so that I might play a part in the finding the right solutions. Joseph would probably chuckle at my soft-handed attempt at shaping the world, but I intend to make it count.

Everything from the alarm clock as large as a sofa to the plastic foot resting on a coffee tin demonstrates the author's penchant for invention. Beyond merely describing the bizarre objects of his imagination, he talks about the creative process. Through the essay, you learn that he is drawn to problem solving, doesn't shy from competition, and loves the possibilities contained in a junky garage.

When your Dragon Does not Breathe Fire

I flick on the light switch, illuminating what must surely be the most baffling garage in Moraga. Huge sheets of plywood lean up against the far wall, a plaster foot rests on a coffee tin full of marbles next to a half-finished dinosaur made of welded steel and coffee filters. I grab a hacksaw and a stack of miniature railroad tracks. As I trim the edges off each piece, my teammates begin to file in, still rubbing the sleep out of their eyes. Few things can drag six teenagers out of bed before noon on President's Day weekend, but Odyssey of the Mind kindles a devotion that challenges most cults. For eight short months, teams from all over the world work to create an eight-minute performance complete with a script, a set, and props. Odyssey of the Mind is a creative problem solving competition that invites imaginative approaches to problem solving. Ever since I was ten years old, the rhythm of my days as well as the habits of my mind have been set by Odyssey's competition calendar.

This year's regional tournament is only a week away, and we are scrambling to complete the centerpiece of our story, an alarm clock the size of a large sofa. Constructed almost exclusively out of our childhood toys and plywood, our clock has a quirky character and a formidable array of pulleys, switches, and conveyor belts that would make Rube Goldberg proud. We spend the day in a trance of painting, gluing, cutting, adjusting and readjusting. Each year, every Odyssey problem unleashes a flood of potential solutions. Our discarded ideas far outnumber our implemented ideas (our dragon never breathed fire out of her nose), but what our brainstorming lacks in practicality it makes up in sheer volume and spontaneity. In the past six years, my team produced a flying carpet, an extendable arm, a giant transforming puzzle cube, and a stomping, roaring ten-foot tall troll.

This process of finding solutions through unrestrained imagination and child-like curiosity is one of the many skills that I developed as I grew up with Odyssey. In Odyssey, there are no dumb questions or wrong answers, and creative risk taking is highly rewarded. I learned that the most readily apparent answers are not necessarily the best ones. I am sure that this perspective of open-ended solutions can be directed to a world faced with seemingly insurmountable problems, from conflict in the Middle East and global warming, to the hunger crisis. Too often our answers are rooted in the past, in the tried and true, or crippled by fear of failure. Conditioned by Odyssey, I am eager to tackle life's problems with creativity and a fresh perspective. I know my effort to address the world issues that I care about may not have the fine storybook ending that Odyssey did – we represented California at the World Finals and received the highest honor, the Ranatra Fusca Award for extraordinary creativity – but as in Odyssey, sometimes it's not the eight-minute performance that matters, it's about walking into the garage at the crack of dawn and seeing the mini-track road of possibilities unfolding before your eyes.

A playful treatment on left-handedness, this essay is both entertaining and clever. The author conveys considerable facility with and love of words, deploying etymologies and unpacking connotations in phrases like "the right way." So, left is sinister and right is always right. As a left-handed author, she charms us into thinking that perhaps left-handedness, far from being a handicap, is a gift. She takes a seemingly trivial topic and turns it into a statement about a defining characteristic.

A Sinister Reflection

It is a wonder, really, what I can do with a pair of hands. With hands, comes the gracing of fingers across the strings of a Celtic harp, slicing the tennis ball to the net. But for me, it also means elbow-nudging the person next to me at the dinner table and awkwardly gripping the handles of scissors. I am left-handed.

I first came down with the case of left-handedness at the age of three. Or, that is when I first noticed I was different. About 7-10 percent of the population is in fact left-handed. I was sad to learn lefties die early. This, of course, is because we are accident-prone. These maladaptive qualities are implied in the word "left-handedness." A synonym for 'left-handedness' is 'sinistrality' from the Latin root *sinestra* meaning sinister. Definitions for "left" range from 'unlucky,' 'improper' to 'immoral.' In short, being 'right' is also the *right* way and the *right* answer and that's *right*.

The metaphors of misfortune aside, there is surprisingly a bright side to being left-handed. Lefties being right-brained are said to be creative. Thus, we're more likely to be innovators. I see biology as story, chemistry as bonding, and literature as blooming. According to neuroscience, this pattern of thinking holds true for many lefties.

Even if left-handedness comes with a string of handicaps, I

am consoled that my condition comes with right-brain domi-
nance. I've got famous lefties such as Bill Gates, Tommy Hilfiger,
Albert Einstein and President Barack Obama on my side. And
hey, at least we lefties are in our *right* minds! So, in my fate-
fully short lifespan, I hope to make something of myself. In my
various decisions and roads ahead of me, I might go the *left*
way instead of the *right* way, but at least, I would leave behind footprints in the road less traveled. And that makes all the
difference.

In this piece, the writer tells a story about how she took a friendship for granted. The main character is likeable because she makes herself vulnerable. In telling the tale of how the lure of winning overtook her, she explains the lesson that friendship is not about utility. The story climaxes with the tragedy that strikes her friend's horse. In its bloody aftermath, she gains some insight about what had been missing in her relationship with Lou. This is an essay about self-discovery.

Lou's Gift

Her head high and eyes wide, Lou sucks in air flaring her nostrils. Her hooves pound with a quick and confident rhythm. With passing years, this image has faded into the background. In its stead, an arena, a stall, and a saddle. Over time, I saw Lou as an instrument and forgot that Lou represents more than the blue ribbons she's earned for me.

Captured by her spirit and beauty, I began riding the Arabian horse at age seven. I loved Lou and cared for her with no concern for a ribbon. Over time and as greater competition ignited my desire for victory, I started to see her as an accessory in my pursuit of the brass ring. That dream was finally reached with two national titles in one year. Perhaps it is human nature to identify someone or something by what it promises to deliver. I started to view my horse as a machine that carries and obeys me, unable at times to see her as constituting more than the assigned role. The best friend I once had withered into a pawn in my pursuit of a national championship.

Ironically, it was the loss of my friend's horse that awakened me to recover my relationship with Lou. Dumbfounded and grief-stricken, I mopped up the animal's blood and tried to console Allison as her horse lay dying. Despite our attempts to save her, the brain aneurism took Phancee's life. I ran blurry eyed to Lou's stall and cried on her shoulder. Her steady breath consoled me. I looked into her eyes and saw only the loving and caring personality she shared with me through my adolescent years. The strong beat of her heart reminded me of the best friend I had forgotten once before but would never forget again.

The next day I ran to Lou's stall. I jumped on her back, no saddle or bridle, and we set out for the open trail. I felt her charge up with life, as we took off to nowhere in particular. We molded together, becoming one again with no intention of turning back.

Through Lou, I learned that when I receive, I must give back. Lou brought back for me what I almost lost when I forgot to heed what makes her tick. She is more than my purveyor of ribbons. We are constantly searching for meaningful relationships, yet they are so hard to maintain. When I look into her big brown eyes, Lou reminds me that nothing trumps this deep connection we have. I will forever be indebted to the friendship Lou has selflessly given me as well as the life lessons she's taught me.

This essay is all in the kick. While there are many essays that center on the spectacular move that lands a win for the team, this one is not about winning as much as it is about the mindset behind the kick. His thesis hinges on the realization: "I hadn't the slightest intention of doing it (scoring)." He goes on to explain that sometimes best things happen when you shut out all the "should's" and just focus on having a good time. The reference "Hakuna Matata" from the Disney film Lion King refers to a philosophy of enjoying the moment.

Hakuna Matata

The stadium lights shined harsh and clean. The crisp evening air gave me goose bumps. I was enjoying the night. As if to shake me out of my reverie, the soccer ball suddenly came rolling towards me. I took my chance and shot it.

The whole thing probably lasted about three seconds, but it felt like both an eternity and a nanosecond. I remember drinking in people's facial expressions as I moved to shoot. The other team tensed up pessimistically while some of my teammates wore expressions you might find on someone watching a favorite vase about to fall. I could hear them yelling for me to pass the ball and I knew they all thought my shot would end up in the field goal. But at that moment, none of it mattered. All I wanted to do was to aim for the goal and kick the ball as hard as I could. And kick it I did. The impact sent a satisfying jolt through my fibula and femur and a resounding "POOM" through the air. To everyone's surprise, the ball soared into the top left corner of the goal. It was a textbook beauty, and I hadn't the slightest intention of doing it.

I replay this moment in my head over and over again. Not for the glory (though I confess to enjoying the applause), but to try and figure out what I did differently that night. I think more than anything it was a change in my mindset. That night, I decided to forget about the game and just play it for the sake of playing. I found myself shielded from the expectations and realities of the game and thus better able to focus on what I was actually doing.

Jonah Lehrer, the author of *Imagine* recommends a "Hakuna Matata" philosophy for problem solving. Although he acknowledges that perseverance and intelligence are important in problem solving, he believes the more difficult problems are best approached slowly and indirectly. As an aspiring engineer, I understand when to muscle my way toward completion and when to just kick back or in this case, kick the ball around. I have learned that the solutions to some of my most challenging problems come to me when I don't chase after them. Rather, a certain level of openness produces better results. When I have to come at something from an unusual angle, I will remember my experience on the soccer field and put aside the pressures of school as well as any fear of failure, and just focus and kick. What I learned that night was that with some things, the reward is all in the doing. Focus, aim, and shoot. That's how I intend to move through life.

In the following piece, the author is responding to a prompt about an object in his room. Because the death of his mother was a life-changing moment for the author, he felt the need to write about how that has shaped his development. Even though the author focuses on a deeply personal tragedy, he achieves a hint of cathartic resolution when he talks about setting his alarm to his favorite radio station. With the alarm turning into song, you get the sense that he is turning over a new chapter.

The Alarm Clock

The faded cream-colored alarm clock sits next to my bed. Every morning with a loud buzz, it beckons me to rise. I have often wondered why I should be so attached to this alarm clock. For, it is neither warm nor fuzzy like a teddy bear. Yet there it sits on my faithful bed stand. It is one of the last items my mother passed on to me.

Over the years, I've come to rely on this alarm clock to get me up every morning. I like to think of the alarm as a personal wake up call from my mother. The word alarm comes from an old Italian noun phrase *all'arme* which means, to arms. It is a call to arm myself against a possible attack. While I hardly think that my days are literal battlefields, there is a sense in which I have to mentally equip myself to face the challenges as well as opportunities put before me every day. That means persevering through the roughest storms.

My mother passed away on June 1, 2005 when I was ten years old. She of all people knew what it meant to fight back. Despite all odds, even when the cancer came around the second time, she refused to give in. All her life my mother had been a hard-working woman. She always told me that I needed to be strong, do my best, and weather any storm. Trying to come to terms with my mother's death was and continues to be the most difficult storm for me. Yet, I have her words and her example as my guide. Thanks to her, I was able to persevere in my most difficult class to date and achieve a high B in AP Chemistry and a 4 on the AP Chemistry exam. Likewise, I know she would have been proud to see me earn my 33 merit badges in Boys Scouts, and ultimately obtain the rank of Eagle Scout, even though it was one of my most challenging and time-consuming endeavors. Lastly, I know that she would be proud to see my dedication to music and seeing me become the first chair French horn player in my school band. As I look ahead to my college days and beyond, I cannot begin to guess what new challenges I will face. But I am learning with each passing day to meet the day with confidence and even joy knowing that I will do my best.

Recently, I've begun to set the alarm to my favorite radio station. In addition to being mentally prepared for my daily challenges, I think my mother would want me to start my day on a happy note.

This is one of my favorite beginnings. The tactile feel of fingernail against plaster is so palpable. The crumbling, decrepit house insinuates the aging uncle holed up inside a timeless mental landscape. In this essay, the author ruminates how only a hairline of a difference separates the insane from the sane. She makes herself vulnerable by daring to make the comparison between herself and her uncle. A keen observer of people with deep empathy, the author writes eloquently about the ways in which we walk around with bleeding hearts.

Saint Sebastian

My mother used to tell me that she could stick her fingernail into the walls of my grandparents' house and the dust from the plaster would come crumbling down. I walked into this same house wearing a Peruvian beanie, the kind of hat with earflaps that dangled down into long, braided strands. "Melissa, your hat reminds me of Tatum O'Neal," greeted my uncle, "Paper Moon. Tatum O'Neal. Her father was Ryan O'Neal. 1973." I listened and smiled.

My uncle never left the house. Dropped out of college. Never married. My mom would often implore, "Van, why can't you help Mother? You could get the mail for her. You can help clean or do the dishes." I thought back to these one-sided conversations, to the stories I heard of how my uncle was harassed and how people would make fun of the way he walked--with his head lowered, mumbling to himself. In school, his classmates broke his school projects and socked him in the eye.

As I walk down my school hallway, I wonder whether the difference between him and me has to do with the extent to which we become detached from reality. I have my moments of losing ground. However, I always come back, with external forces guiding and encouraging me, rather than giving me bruised eyes. Perhaps the key to understanding my uncle is making real the absence of reality—making sense of the thoughts I try to abandon.

People have warned me of my own habits toward disassociation. As I walk about school, my mind often freezes in front of something captivating—maybe the expression on Saint Sebastian's face and the startling red dripping over his body. Sentenced to execution by arrows, Sebastian beseechingly looks skyward, yet somehow he does not die, even with arrowheads piercing his body. It is not necessarily the plot that makes Sebastian so beautiful, but rather Mantegna's portrayal of the idea. He is a man anticipating death. He finds himself at death's threshold, walking through earth with arrows in his heart. "I feel frozen, trapped in a brick— a brick of ice… for 7 hours straight. Just standing," writes Sebastian on the eve of his death. Perhaps my uncle is thinking of something beautiful—something that may consume precisely 7 hours to contemplate, too precious to pause for later.

In a sense, we are all a little like Saint Sebastian. I often say that the most uncomfortable position to be in is life. I chuckle as my peers walk to class as if arrows have been pierced directly into their guts. However anxious I feel about pain, I can still accept it and smile-- pain representing a point of reflection and progress. This is another difference between my uncle and me. Saint Sebastian to me is a reminder of the pain we feel as what defines life. Somehow, the strength and recovery from pain can make the blood look beautiful. To my Uncle, Saint Sebastian would represent horror and isolation. I have often thought of myself as immoral, needing to correct my own thoughts and veil any horror and isolation. But at other times, I cannot hide from the pain. I realize that all people have this Saint Sebastian within them, those vicious thoughts that for some reason wish to live on despite the extraordinary pain they bring. Then I see my uncle as Saint Sebastian, still walking even with arrows in his heart.

A friend of mine once said, "People like us are obsessed with meaning." I see the foundation of my grandparents' house, crumbling with my uncle trapped inside. I see Saint Sebastian in my peers. I want to understand those who desperately need to be understood. College offers this chance for me to give and receive. I want to be surrounded by people who not only acknowledge the ups and downs of friendships, but understand them as well, even if it does mean finding the truth so blinding it hurts to look.

The author of this essay initially did not see herself as a writer. After many drafts that refused to breathe, she finally gave birth to a live one. Lacking in her early attempts was a sense of being transformed by an experience. Her inability to let herself go kept her from writing well. At first, it was very difficult for her to admit to this failing but as she testifies in the story, her little sister in pigtails taught her how. Learning to relax has enabled the author to write with considerable charm and humor. Consequently, her voice comes through beautifully in this essay.

Teacher in Pigtails

Gazing out the car window, she asked, "When do trees sleep? They are always standing." Dumbfounded, I began to wonder why after so many years of looking at trees, such a thought never crossed my mind. Abby, my four-year-old sister never fails to surprise me with her mind-blowing observations. Hers is a world of unceasing enchantment.

And here I am, pouring over such exotic curios like SAT practice tests, memorizing words like, "dowager" and "interlocutor." My personal favorite is "maelstrom"—an apt description of my life as a high school student, sucked into an overwhelming vortex of work pushing me around in ten directions at once. And there are days I ask, *What's it all about?* Recently, I was asked to explain the significance of "letting go." Clearly, such a concept did not exist in my life. "Letting go is uhhhh…" I stumbled, "the ability uh… to completely live in the moment, letting go of the past and the future?" As I explained this peculiar concept, a lump rose to my throat and a haze over my eyes as I looked out into the green hills. Trying to get my leg up on the competition, I am wondering if I am winning—or losing?

My little sister has taught me to put the varoom back into learning. Work is play and play is work. Happiness, Presence, and Creativity are her motto. Life is one fascinating encounter after another. She does things because she derives pleasure from doing them, not worrying about the consequences or the rewards. Thinking about the fruits of tomorrow has inhibited me from tasting the flavors of today.

My sister is my Zen master. Every day with her perky questions about sleeping trees or the witchy moon, she teaches me the importance of play. She has made me realize that playing is as essential as breathing. Even with my schedule, I now seek to enjoy what I am doing. As I enter into college, a new outlook toward life accompanies me, one in which harmonizing play and work will hopefully unleash a whole new way of seeing, learning, and discovering.

Here is another essay focused on an object. An object with emotive significance lends itself nicely to the personal essay. While the unfolding story takes place in the space of a day, its significance lasts a lifetime as she reflects on its meaning. Her reference to the root meaning of "merry" as brief is particularly apt in describing the metaphor of childhood and the fleeting image of a carousel going round and round. Key to an excellent essay is coming up with apt metaphors.

The Carousel

The blue and lavender box caught his eye. He picked it up, twisted the little nob, and watched the white horses go round and round. I had to laugh a little at the idea of receiving a music box for my fifteenth birthday. The self-conscious, sheepish smile on his face was enough to expose his endearingly irrational desire to arrest me in childhood and keep me spinning on the merry-go-round forever. As an afterthought, he bought another ticket for me. "Come on, you won't be a kid forever!" he half-joked as he handed me the red stub. I clambered on next to my little brother and watched my dad's beaming face fly by as the merry-go-round spun and the horses went up and down. "Merry" comes from a proto-Germanic word meaning "brief" or "short-lasting," and both Dad and I felt the poignantly ephemeral beauty of that day at the merry-go-round. For one eternal moment I was carried back to the exuberance and exhilaration of childhood.

As I prepare to step off the merry-go-round and enter adulthood, I know I will never forget that sense of wonderment and elation I felt whirling around on the carousel. Far from leaving it behind, growing up has meant never letting go of my childish openness and spontaneity. Although the phrase "child's play" typically describes an activity that is thoughtless and trivial, children play with intent seriousness fully present to the moment. I am still enthralled by the gunpowder sky just before a storm and the blank potential of a snow covered field. Imagination is the precursor to perception.

When Dad bought the mini carousel that day, he meant it as a tribute to the aching loveliness of that moment, expressive of a bittersweet nostalgia for a childhood passing all too quickly. But to me it is more than a simple nostalgia piece. It is a reminder to keep playing, to be open to amazement, to laugh defiantly in the face of that ridiculously rational warning; "You won't be a kid forever!" Childhood is not a stage of life. It is a state of mind.

Rather than focus on books by usual suspects like Hemingway or Fitzgerald, the author of this essay chooses to reflect on a stanza from her favorite childhood poet. Looking at the poem anew as a young adult spurs new thinking for her. I am drawn to the powerful imagery she paints in her opening paragraph such as the "jagged piece of gray cement," "the purple mantle of possibilities," or "the geometric civility of neat sidewalks." But don't let her poetic prose fool you, for, beneath the seductive imagery lies an incisive and persuasive argument that science is in fact creative. The unusual pairing of creativity and science makes this a unique essay.

Where the Sidewalk Ends

There is a place where the sidewalk ends
And before the street begins,
And there the grass grows soft and white,
And there the sun burns crimson bright
             -Shel Silverstein, Where the Sidewalk Ends

The sidewalk ends at the edge of reality, where the last jagged piece of gray cement juts out over a purple mantel of possibilities. Here the harsh lines of reality blur and bleed together with imagination; the façade is stripped away to unveil the truth. Truth is elegant and simple; we know it by its striking clarity and grace. Truth resonates. Silverstein abandons the artifice of appearance, of mere factuality, that so often prevents us from seeing the naked essence. He invites us to look beyond the geometric civility of neat sidewalks. In order to discover anything new, we too must stand on the precipitous edge and set our eyes on what lies beyond. Often times we find truth disconcerting and uncomfortable, because it is unfamiliar and bizarre. It takes us by surprise and forces us to confront the flaws in the prevailing theory, to challenge that which is law. In short, we must move beyond the accepted, the familiar, risking everything in search of the truth.

I am a scientist, and this advice may sound peculiar coming from someone who works with empirically proven data. It is easy to assume that in science the established facts reign supreme and there are certain rules that cannot be bent or broken. However, I see science as a profoundly creative process. The beauty of science is not so much found in the individual facts and figures, but in the synthesis, the unifying theory that is woven from seemingly disparate pieces of evidence. It takes imagination to find the thread that connects the data; to tease it out, scientists must be willing to break with convention and look at the problem from a new angle. This process cannot be bound by history, but should always look to future possibilities. Those who went beyond the most obvious solutions and ventured into the realm of the improbable have made great discoveries. When scientists first detected spongiform encephalopathies, such as mad cow disease and scrapie, many thought that they were caused by genetic mutations, a likely hypothesis because mutated DNA caused many other neurodegenerative diseases. However, in the 1960s scientists Alper and Griffith began to gather evidence that pointed to a protein carrier of the disease rather than a nucleic acid carrier. Later, scientists built upon their theory, and in 1982 the prion (a misfolded protein) was purified and identified as an infectious agent.

The solutions to today's dilemmas likewise depend upon such ingenuity.

In my approach to science and to life in general, Silverstein's call for open-mindedness and originality is a guiding force. "Where the Sidewalk Ends" is a refreshing reminder that in a world where fixed reality tends to dominate our thinking process, we cannot lose sight of creativity that inspire progress and new discovery.

A mark of a good essay is its ability to make you fall a little in love with its author. Anyone who would think to ask for a blank trophy and write about it is endearing. What school wouldn't die to have a student who needs no rewards for her achievements and for whom every endeavor is a work in progress! In this deceptively insouciant story about a blank trophy, you in fact learn a great deal about the author's values and the lens by which she views the world. I also appreciate the way the author turns the empty trophy this way and that, rendering it from various angles and dimensions to bring out a nuanced discussion about the meaning of work.

A Blank Trophy

Jealous of my brother who participated in Little League, I asked my parents if I too could have a trophy. The thought of awards enticed me. I didn't understand completely what awards were for, but it seemed that they were like prizes. I felt embarrassed when I opened my present. It was what I asked for, but not what I wanted. A blank trophy with no honors or praises.

My trophy is silent and clear. Physically free of words and images, my trophy is angular and made of glass, open to reflection and reaction, which stems from simple acts of creating. It sits on a shelf and remains in the same position, with dust caking my view of it at times. I only realize now that a trophy serves no purpose for me. It does not reflect thoughts. Why do I need an emblem that stands for achievement or success if I am constantly evolving, always an unfinished product? For me, the process of getting there is more important. I would like a trophy filled with space, with room to swirl and change. My empty trophy is a reminder that individual creation is a long and arduous process.

For some reason, the world that I live in likes to point to the trophies labeled "MVP of the year" as if a single goal will be satisfying enough. However, satisfaction diffuses. This is why it is important to constantly be "reinventing yourself" as Pablo Picasso says, to keep a torch always in hand to fire new distortions, never copying what we already have established of ourselves. While I play in this infinite jungle of identity, I recreate and reflect on my bindings. I can begin to understand the dichotomy between others and myself. We think so differently, yet on some underlying, interpersonal level, if I understand my own wanderings, then I can open up and accept difference in others around me. In me there are bits and pieces of the world swirling around and when I connect with one aspect, I am taking note of that piece of myself in others. When I asked for a trophy, I think more than anything I wanted to be seen and to see others as they are. This lies at the center of everything I strive to do.

Bibliography (Works Used)

Amabile, Teresa M. *The Social Psychology of Creativity*. New York: Springer-Verlag Press, 1983.

Arum, Richard and Josipa Roksa. *Academically Adrift: Limited Learning on College Campuses*. Chicago: University of Chicago Press, 2010.

Baldwin, James. "Notes of a Native Son." In *The Art of the Personal Essay: An Anthology from the Classical Era to the Present*. Edited by Phillip Lopate. New York: Anchor Books, 1995: 586-604.

Barzun, Jacques. *Simple & Direct: A Rhetoric for Writers*. New York: Harper Perennial, 2002.

Bender, Sheila, *Keeping a Journal You Love*. Cincinnati: Walking Stick Press, 2001.

Byum, Caroline Walker. "Presidential Address." *The American Historical Review*. February 1997: 1-26.

Colvin, Geoff. *Talent Is Overrated*. New York: Penguin Books, 2008.

Csikszentmihalyi, Mihaly. *Creativity: Flow and the Psychology of Discovery and Invention.* New York: Haper Collings Publishers, 1996.

Dewey, John. *Freedom and Culture.* Buffalo, New York: Prometheus Books, 1989.

Dillard, Annie. "Seeing." In *The Art of the Personal Essay: An Anthology from the Classical Era to the Present.* Edited by Phillip Lopate. New York: Anchor Books, 1995: 692-706.

Dweck, Carol. *Mindset: the New Psychology of Success.* New York: Ballantine Books, 2006.

Flaherty, Alice W. *The Midnight Disease: The Drive to Write, Writer's Block, and the Creative Brain.* Boston: Houghton Mifflin Company, 2005.

Flink, William, Addison Hibbard. *Handbook to Literature.* New York: Odyssey Press, 1960, 349.

Forche, Carolyn and Philip Gerard, Eds. *Writing Creative Nonfiction.* Cincinnati: Story Press, 2001.

Frankl, Viktor E. *Man's Search for Meaning: An Introduction to Logotherapy.* New York: Simon & Schuster, Inc., 1984.

Franzen, Jonathan. "My Father's Brain." In *How To Be Alone: Essays.* New York: Farrar, Straus, and Giroux, 2002: 7-38.

Goleman, Daniel. *Emotional Intelligence: Why It Can Matter More than IQ.* New York: Bantam Books, 1995.

Gutkind, Lee. Ed. *The Best Creative Nonfiction*. New York: W.W. Norton and Company, 2009.

_____*You Can't Make This Stuff up: the Complete Guide to Writing Creative Nonfiction*. Boston: Da Capo Press, 2012.

Hong Kingston, Maxine. *The Woman Warrior: Memoirs of a Girlhood among Ghosts*. New York: Alfred A. Knopf, 1976.

Johnson, Samuel. *Selected Essays from the Rambler, Adventurer & Idler*. New Haven: Yale University Press, 1968.

Kaufman, Scott Barry and James C. Kaufman. *Psychology of Creative Writing*. Cambridge: Cambridge University Press, 2009.

Kooser, Ted. *The Poetry Home Repair Manual*. Lincoln, Nebraska: University of Nebraska Press, 2005.

Kuusisto, Stephen. *Eavesdropping: A Memoir of Blindness and Listening*. New York: W.W. Norton and Company, 2006.

Lamott, Anne. *Bird by Bird: Some Instructions on Writing and Life*. New York: First Anchor Books, 1995.

Lehrer, Jonah. *Imagine: How Creativity Works*. New York: Houghton Mifflin Harcourt Press, 2012.

Lopate, Phillip. *Getting Personal: Selected Essays*. New York: Basic Books, 2003.

Lopate, Phillip. *To Show and to Tell: the Craft of Literary Nonfiction*. New York: Free Press, 2013.

MacLeish, Archibald. *"Ars Poetica."* In *The Poetry Anthology, 1912-2002*. Edited by Joseph Parisi and Stephen Young. Chicago: Ivan R. Dee, 2002: 61.

Moore, Dinty W. *Crafting the Personal Essay: A Guide for Writing and Publishing Creative Nonfiction*. Cincinnati: Writer's Digest Books, 2010.

Murphy, Daniel. *Martin Buber's Philosophy of Education*. Dublin: Irish Academic Press, 1988.

Pink, Daniel H. *A Whole New Mind: Why Right-Brainers Will Rule the Future*. New York: Riverhead Books, 2005.

_____ *Drive: the Surprising Truth about What Motivates Us*. New York: Riverhead House, 2010.

Prose, Francine. *Reading Like a Writer: A Guide for People Who Love Books and for Those Who Want to Write Them*. New York: Harper Perennial, 2006.

Provost, Gary. *100 Ways to Improve Your Writing*. New York: New American Library, 1985.

Ross, Brian H. Ed. *The Psychology of Learning and Motivation: Advances in Research and Theory*. Volume 49. Boston: Elsevier Press, 2008.

Selgin, Peter. *By Cunning and Craft: Sound Advice and Practical Wisdom for Fiction Writers*. Cincinnati: Writer's Digest Books, 2007.

Sims, Patsy. Edited. *Literary Nonfiction: Learning by Example.* New York: Oxford University Press, 2002.

Sorrentino, Richard M. and Susuma Yamaguchi. Eds. *Handbook of Motivation and Cognition Across Cultures.* San Francisco: Academic Press, 2008.

Strunk Jr., William and E.B. White. *The Elements of Style*, 4th Edition. New York: Macmillan Press, 2000.

Tharp, Twyla. *The Creative Habit: Learn It and Use It for Life.* New York: Simon & Schuster, 2003.

Wagner, Hugh. *The Psychobiology of Human Motivation.* New York: Routlege, 1999.

Wigfield, Allan and Jacquelynne S. Eccles. Eds. *Development of Achievement Motivation,* A volume in the Educational Psychology Series. San Diego: Academic Press, 2001.

Williams, Joseph M. *Style: Ten Lessons in Clarity and Grace.* 7th Edition. New York: Addison-Wesley Educational Publishers, Inc. 2003.

CPSIA information can be obtained
at www.ICGtesting.com
Printed in the USA
FSHW021323291019
63518FS